Turning *for* Furniture

Turning *for* Furniture

CREATING FURNITURE
PARTS ON YOUR LATHE

Ernie Conover

The Taunton Press

Taunton
BOOKS & VIDEOS
for fellow enthusiasts

First printing: 1996
Printed in the United States of America

A FINE WOODWORKING Book
FINE WOODWORKING® is a trademark of The Taunton Press, Inc.,
registered in the U.S. Patent and Trademark Office.

The Taunton Press, 63 South Main Street,
Box 5506, Newtown, CT 06470-5506

Library of Congress Cataloging-in-Publication Data

Conover, Ernie.
        Turning for Furniture: creating furniture parts
        on your lathe /Ernie Conover:
        drawings by Robert La Pointe
            p.   cm.
        "A Fine Woodworking book" — T.p. verso.
        Includes index.
        ISBN 1-56158-117-8
        1. Turning.   2. Furniture making.
        I. Title.
        TT202.C66   1996   96-22633
        684'.08 — dc20   CIP

To my children: Charles, Anne, Genoa and Justin.

ACKNOWLEDGMENTS

I would like to acknowledge the following friends and colleagues who were most helpful with information and tireless in reviewing text: Sam Barrens (Woodcraft Supply), Tim Clay (Oneway Manufacturing), Mike Dunbar, Jerry Glaser (Glaser Engineering), Dave Hout, Brian Latimer (Nova Chuck), Anthony LeClerc (General Manufacturing Co., Ltd.), Leonard Lee (Lee Valley Tools and author of *The Complete Guide to Sharpening*), Richard Lukes (Beech Street Tool Works), Gerald Motley (Powermatic Corp.), Darel Nish (Craft Supplies USA), Rude Osolnik, Brad Packard (Packard WoodWorks), Mark Schiefer (Delta International), Mark Williams (Veritas Tools, Inc.) and Russ Zimmerman.

CONTENTS

INTRODUCTION

In this book I would like to share with you some of the joy I get from making furniture with parts that I have turned myself. While there are numerous books about turning, there are none that deal with turning as an important aspect of furniture making. Instead, most lathe books deal with turning as a pursuit unto itself and overlook the important techniques (especially duplication) needed by the furniture maker to make small production runs from two to a hundred or so pieces. Most recent texts cater to the hobbyist turner interested in producing art exclusively with the lathe and dwell on faceplate work, mainly bowls. What differentiates this book from the rest is that it looks closely at the practical (and possibly profitable) turning needs of the furniture maker and disregards art turning.

Sooner or later most furniture makers want to incorporate turnings in their work. This first attempt at turning is often a table or chair leg. I feel it is important that this first turning experience be positive, because one's future attitudes toward turning will be set by this first session. The purpose of this book is to make turning an enjoyable part of the furniture production process. I will show you how to start with the proper tools (that are sharp and ground to the correct shape) and how to use proven techniques that will give you good results—right from the start.

I must add, however, that the best lathe, tools and techniques will not make you a proficient turner. Turning is a skill, and just as in playing a sport or a musical instrument, it takes commitment, patience and practice to achieve proficiency. Learning involves making mistakes. To become competent you must find the limits. You will only know how far you can roll a gouge by rolling it until it catches. It is best to do some practice turning *before* you start working on furniture parts. If you're a beginner, one or more practice parts should be turned from scrap wood before you attempt to turn the finished product.

This book is really a detailed shop reference guide on how to turn all the common, and a good many uncommon, furniture components. It covers the fine nuances of tools, chucking, duplicating and sanding. For those who have had a bad experience turning, I hope you can "turn the other cheek" and reacquaint yourself with your lathe. Remember, the more you practice, the better you will get.

Part One

THE BASICS

What You Need in a Lathe

Before you can consider incorporating turnings in furniture, you need a lathe and the necessary tools and accessories. How good a lathe you need will depend largely on the scale, volume and type of furniture you plan to produce. While very little is needed in a lathe for light spindle work, heavy faceplate work (such as outboard turning of tabletops) and large spindle work (such as bed posts, newel posts and table bases) require a lathe of robust construction.

One of the best ways to identify a solid, well-made lathe is to look at the materials used to construct it. Most lathes today are made entirely from metal. My first choice is an all cast-iron machine. Often other materials are substituted for cast iron in an effort to bring a more reasonably priced machine to the marketplace. The most common way to cut costs is to substitute other materials in the bed (typically structural steel). Another common material for bed rails is aluminum. These are expensive and don't possess the vibration-damping or strength characteristics that I look for and so should be avoided.

Another critical consideration is the type of bearings in the headstock. You'll find sleeve-type, ball or roller bearings. Sleeve bearings were used extensively in economy lathes in the past. But advances in ball-bearing manufacture have all but eliminated sleeve bearings in lathe construction. With ball bearings, a single row is adequate, but a double row offers better support for a lathe spindle.

Manufacturers save money by placing a double-row bearing at the front and a single row at the back, where there is less radial pressure. (Used lathes with sleeve bearings are probably best avoided.)

Lathe Types

Lathes can be divided into roughly three categories of the work they're able to handle—light, medium and heavy duty.

A light-duty lathe is often all that is necessary for the small-scale furniture maker. A typical light-duty model is adequate for such tasks as the turning of chair or table legs, knobs and finials. Better models are even adequate for medium faceplate work, such as a stool seat. But with inexpensive bearings, lack of index head, limited distance between centers and overall light weight, this is about all any light-duty lathe can handle.

A medium-duty lathe is the best choice for most furniture makers. A medium-duty lathe has better bearings and more weight, as well as greater distance between centers, an index head and a heavy, easy-to-

Lathe-Buying Criteria			
Feature	Light Duty	Medium Duty	Heavy Duty
Construction	Hybrid of cast iron, structural steel, aluminum extrusions and liberal use of plastic.	Mainly cast iron but often with structural steel bed. Some use of aluminum extrusions and/or plastic.	Usually solid cast iron, although structural steel bed is occasionally seen. Little use of aluminum or plastic.
Bearings	Sleeve or ball.	Ball, with front spindle bearing sometimes being double-row ball bearing.	Double-row ball bearing on front and back, or occasionally roller bearings.
Weight	Less than 250 lb.	200 lb. to 400 lb.	Over 400 lb.
Swing	8 in. to 12 in.	10 in. to 12 in.	12 in. to 20 in. or more.
Distance between centers	29 in. to 36 in.	29 in. to 39 in.	38 in. or more with bed extensions.
Index head	None.	8, 24 or 60.	24 or 60.

move tool rest that allows you to tackle any turning—spindle or faceplate. Most medium-duty models will turn medium to large tabletops outboard with the aid of a floor-stand tool rest.

A heavy-duty lathe is the logical choice for the professional furniture maker or anyone who enjoys owning the best. Heavy-duty lathes are solid and vibration-free, and tool rests move with great ease. Many models have provisions for an outboard rest that attaches to the machine itself to allow for large outboard turnings—diameters of 22 in. to 40 in.—without having to resort to a floor-stand tool rest (see photo, p. 8). The weight of a heavy-duty lathe is of particular advantage in turning large tabletops (especially outboard) and large spindles, such as table bases, newel posts or bed posts.

Lathe Features

Whether you decide to go with a light-, medium- or heavy-duty lathe, there are a few features you should pay particular attention to: the type of spindle, the index head, the distance between centers, the swing, the outboard-turning capabilities and the range of speeds.

The Record Coronet No. 1 is a good light-duty benchtop lathe. (Photo courtesy of Record Tools, Inc.)

The Delta 46-700 is a medium-duty lathe well-suited to the needs of most furniture makers. It is adequate for spindle work, and the swing-head design allows reasonable size faceplate work.

The Delta Top Turn 16 is a heavy-duty lathe with a modular cast-iron bed design and a large outboard-turning capacity.

SPINDLE TYPE

A salient feature of any lathe worthy of consideration by a serious craftsman is one that has hollow spindles designed to accept Morse-taper sockets in both the headstock and tailstock. Morse tapers lock in place when inserted into the matching tapered socket in the spindle. This allows for quick and easy mounting of drive centers and a host of other accessories. Morse tapers lock when driven home and release with an equal opposite force. They're universal, so you're not dependent on the manufacturer for replacement accessories (for more on Morse tapers, see p. 118).

INDEX HEAD

Some headstocks are fitted with an index head, which is a mechanism that allows the spindle to be locked at equal intervals so that layout or auxiliary operations can be performed. An example of such an operation is milling reeds or flutes in a column by hand or with a router (see Chapter 8). The most common setup for indexing is a series of holes drilled in the back of the headstock drive pulley, which is mounted to the spindle. A pin in the headstock casting slides into the appropriate hole and locks the spindle in place. Common hole patterns are 12, 24 and 60. I like the 24-stop configuration because it allows me to divide the circumference of a workpiece into eight equal parts (an octagon is a common period-furniture shape). For certain types of furniture, such as fluted legs, this feature is essential.

DISTANCE BETWEEN CENTERS

Distance between centers is also important. While 36 in. is adequate for most furniture parts, 38 in. (or more) is nice to have. For the once-in-a-lifetime long project, it's usually possible to rig an extension of some sorts to the bed or to make the turning in sections. But if long work is to be commonplace, a long bed is a must. With some lathe models, you can purchase optional bed extensions that allow you to add extra length when needed. Other lathes are designed with a wood bed, which can be made to any reasonable length.

SWING

Swing is a much bandied term in lathe advertisements. It's an attempt to give the buyer an idea of the maximum diameter that the machine can handle. By definition, swing is twice the center height (the distance from the actual bed to the center of the spindle). But the true capacity of a lathe is not the swing but rather the diameter that can be accommodated over the tool base (which holds the tool rest). This true capacity can be calculated by deducting twice the tool-base height from the swing. For example, most tool bases are between 1 in. and 1½ in. in height, so the swing is reduced by 2 in. to 3 in.

For spindle turning (which covers the majority of furniture-making situations), a great amount of swing is not necessary. In fact, an 8-in. swing (which usually yields about 6 in. over the tool rest) can be quite adequate. There are a number of small swing-head lathes with capacities in this range. This will handle most spindle turning, while the swing head allows faceplate work up to the size of stool seats.

Some manufacturers try to increase swing by building a "gap" in the bed of the lathe. While this does allow for larger faceplate work, it's actually a hindrance for spindle work. Because it is impossible to place the tool base in the gap, there is a large "blind spot" where the tool rest cannot be positioned. This makes working on the backside of a piece mounted on a faceplate impossible, and most spindle work inconvenient. The solution is to purchase a gap filler (if the lathe manufacturer offers one) or to fabricate one yourself. The gap may be filled quite adequately with wood by drilling and tapping holes in the gap and attaching the wood with countersunk machine screws.

OUTBOARD TURNING

Outboard turning with a floor-stand tool rest deserves some mention here. A floor-stand tool rest is simply a steel column with a heavy tripod base that accepts the various tool rests that normally fit into the tool base during inboard turning (see photo at right). Floor-stand tool rests do not have the rigidity of a normal tool base, especially on large-diameter work, such as tabletops. If you try normal shear-cutting techniques, the leverage required will usually tip the floor-stand tool rest. Consequently, this rest can be a bit dangerous. Floor-stand tool rests should be used with a good deal of caution and only with light scraping cuts.

The distance between centers on some lathes can be increased by adding optional bed extensions.

Because a floor-stand rest does not have the rigidity of a normal tool base, it should be used only with light scraping cuts.

Some lathes offer a second outboard tool base that attaches to the bed casting (or the base of the lathe). This allows turning outboard of large faceplate work (22 in. to 40 in., depending on the make of the lathe) off the back end of the spindle but retains the rigidity of inboard turning (see left photo, facing page). In such arrangements the back end of the spindle is left-hand threaded, with the same pitch and diameter thread as the spindle nose. The left-hand thread keeps the faceplate from unscrewing during operation. Because the work is turning in the opposite direction on the outboard side, outboard turning is a mirror image of inboard turning. The disadvantage to this system is that you may need to purchase a set of left-hand faceplates for outboard turning. (Delta is an exception because its faceplates have both left- and right-hand threads.)

A variation of this arrangement is to have a pivoting headstock (called a swing head), which can be turned at right angles to the bed (see right photo, facing page). With this feature, larger-diameter faceplate work can be swung in front of the bed, and the normal tool base can be used with an extension casting. The swing-head arrangement seems to be a new trend in light- and medium-duty lathes. It allows good-size faceplate work in a lathe of modest center height. One of the biggest advantages of the swing-head design is that you can use your normal right-hand faceplates instead of buying an additional set of left-hand ones, which can be expensive.

SPEED
The range and ease of changing speeds on a lathe is an important feature worthy of close attention. There are three ways to vary the speed of a lathe: with a step pulley, a variable-width pulley or a DC motor. Each has its advantages and disadvantages.

Step pulley
The original drive system for connecting a lathe to a power source was a flat leather belt. A three- or four-step set of matched pulleys gave a range of speed for the turner. Modern lathes utilize V-belts and pulleys for better power transmission. They're reliable and inexpensive. The disadvantage is that to change speeds, you have to turn off the lathe and move the V-belt from one pulley to another by hand. Add to this the limited range of incremental speeds, and it's readily apparent why most turners prefer a variable-speed lathe.

Variable-width pulley
To create a wider range of speeds, some lathe manufacturers provide a variable-width pulley system. A mechanical control adjusts the width of the pulley, which effectively changes the diameter and speed. Moving the two halves of the drive pulley apart decreases the

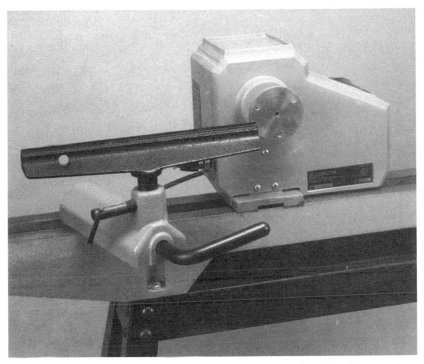

An outboard tool base on some lathes allows turning of large faceplate work off the back end of the spindle, with the rigidity of inboard turning.

A lathe with a swing-head design allows you to pivot the headstock at a right angle to the bed so that you can turn in front of the lathe. The normal tool base can be used with an extension casting.

diameter and speed; squeezing the halves back together does the reverse. This system allows "on-the-fly" speed changes, along with a range of infinitely variable speeds. The only disadvantage to this system is increased wear on the belts and the mechanical parts of the lathe and the expenses.

DC motors

Increasingly, manufacturers are putting DC (direct current) motors with solid-state controls on lathes. Today's solid-state circuitry allows controls that make DC current from ordinary single-phase household current. This makes it possible simply to dial a speed, which is more convenient than moving a belt by hand to change speed. The one disadvantage to the DC motor is its high cost

Recommended speeds

One question that comes up repeatedly in my workshops is what speeds are best for turning. The answer will depend on the type of turning. For spindle turning up to 2½ in. in diameter (furniture spindles), a roughing speed of about 1,100 rpm and a finished speed of about 1,700 rpm are appropriate. An experienced turner will be able to do the entire operation at the higher speed, as long as the work is well-centered to begin with.

Faceplate turning calls for slower speeds. For work up to 10 in. in diameter, 600 to 800 rpm is a good roughing speed; 1,100 rpm is an appropriate finishing speed. Faceplate work need never be done at a speed greater than 1,100 rpm. For large-diameter faceplate work (such as a tabletop), speeds as low as 200 rpm may be necessary.

All lathes come with one or two tool rests, usually 6 in. and 12 in. long. The 6 in. rest is reserved for small work, like knobs and finials, and the 12-in. rest is used most of the time.

Tool Rests for Furniture Parts

All lathes come with one or two standard tool rests, typically 6 in. and 12 in. long. The 12-in. tool rest is used most of the time, with the 6-in. tool rest usually reserved for small work, such as knobs and finials. Because most furniture parts are longer than 12 in., a turner will have to reposition the tool base one or more times during the turning process. While this may not seem important, constantly moving the tool rest as you work along a spindle really is a hassle. It's especially a problem when you're trying to smooth a long cylinder or taper a leg.

The remedy is a longer tool rest. Many lathe manufacturers offer an 18-in. tool rest, which is handy because it allows turning most parts without moving the tool base more than once during a single turning. Also available are 36-in. tool rests, but these have two necks and so require two tool bases. However, if you plan on turning long spindles often, the additional expense of the 36-in. tool rest and its two tool bases is money well-spent.

In addition to length, it's also important to look closely at the tool base for the rest and its locking mechanism. The tool base must lock down securely and not slide under a load. The hold-down/locking mechanisms range from wedges under the bed that are pounded snug with a mallet, to a simple nut and bolt that are tightened with a wrench, to complicated lever-operated cam mechanisms. With each level of sophistication comes a commensurate increase in price. When choosing a lathe, the best course is to try the tool base and see how it operates: Move it to a variety of angles and positions, lock it in place, grab it with both hands and see if you can move it.

FULL-LENGTH TOOL RESTS

The most obvious benefit of a full-length tool rest is that no movement of the rest is necessary (with the possible exception of sliding it a bit forward between roughing and finishing). Less obvious is that duplication is much easier. By applying masking tape to the tool rest, critical points on a spindle can be marked so that the tool rest becomes a measuring, or "story," stick, and you won't need to refer constantly to rulers and dividers.

It is possible to make your own full-length tool rest from wood (see drawing below). All that's required is to find a suitable spot on your tailstock casting to drill and tap a hole for the hardware. This allows a wood tool rest of any length up to about 40 in. to be attached. The tools will dent the wood, but this does not cause the slightest problem, if you've used a hardwood such as oak or maple and if the top edge of the tool rest is sloped like that in the drawing. The tools used for detail turning (which are mostly spindle gouges) will contact the very edge of the tool rest, while the tools used for cutting long cylinders and tapers (the roughing-out gouge and the skew) will

SHOPMADE FULL-LENGTH TOOL REST

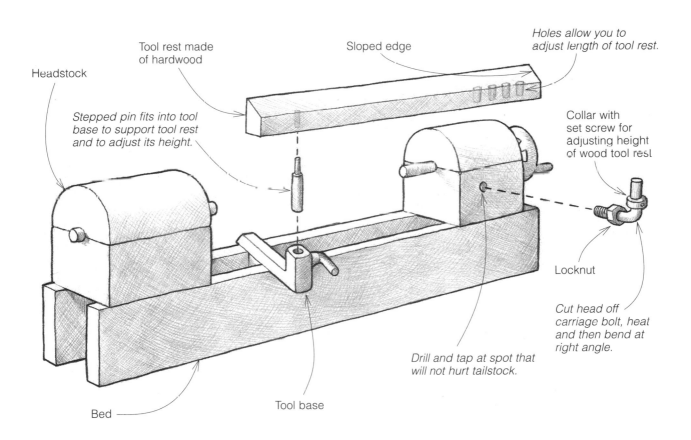

Tool rest made of hardwood

Sloped edge

Holes allow you to adjust length of tool rest.

Headstock

Stepped pin fits into tool base to support tool rest and to adjust its height.

Collar with set screw for adjusting height of wood tool rest

Locknut

Cut head off carriage bolt, heat and then bend at right angle.

Drill and tap at spot that will not hurt tailstock.

Bed

Tool base

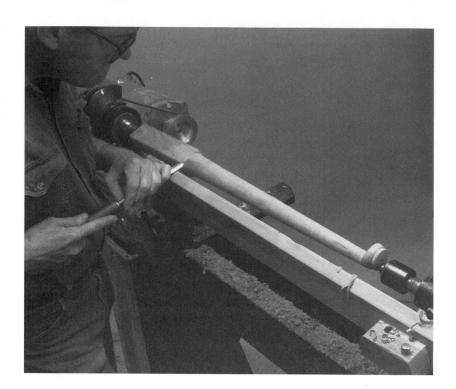

A full-length wood tool rest is simple to make (see drawing on p. 13) and allows you to draw lines on it at critical points. Also, the dents made by the detail tools actually help the tools to "know" where to go, which aids in duplication.

contact just behind the edge of the tool rest. The wood tool rest allows you to draw pencil lines on it at critical points, and the dents made by the detail tools actually help the duplication process. After four or five spindles, the tools sort of "know" where to go.

STEADY RESTS

When a long spindle becomes thin, it starts to vibrate between centers, like a string on a musical instrument. The result is harmonic "chatter," often called "barber-poling." Whatever name, this phenomenon shows up as spiral ridges on the spindle. Harmonic chatter is more pronounced at the center of the spindle (where it bends the easiest) than at the ends. It can be eliminated, or at least minimized, through the use of a steady rest. A steady rest supports the work at the center, dampening vibration in much the same way a musician silences a string by placing his finger on it. With a steady rest, roughing goes faster because much heavier cuts may be taken without the spindle bowing and popping out of the lathe. Commercial steady rests are available, but it is a simple matter to make one (see drawing, facing page).

You might think that a steady rest must contact the work at three places and hold it dead on center. Actually, only two contact points are necessary. And it doesn't even matter if the steady rest pushes the work slightly off center. In fact, I've found that this arrangement works better to dampen vibration.

If the workpiece becomes hot and starts to burn as a result of it rubbing against the notch, use wax as a lubricant and reduce the lathe speed. I have also screwed strips of Teflon to the steady rest with good results. Another method that has proven effective is to wrap the spindle with Teflon plumber's tape at the point of contact with the steady rest.

SHOPMADE STEADY REST

Use available hardwood or high grade of plywood (or combination of the two).

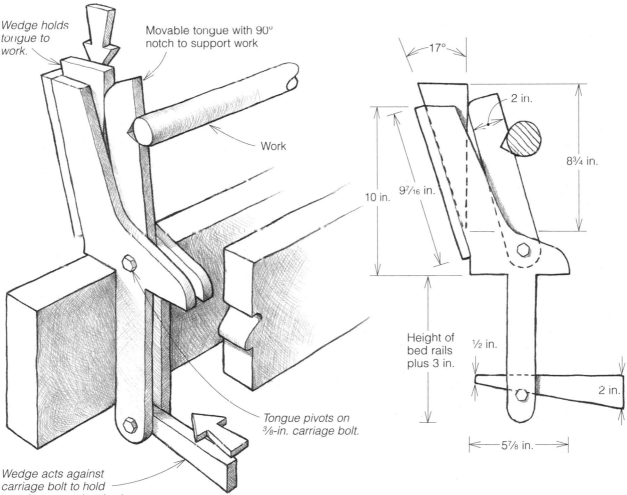

Wedge holds tongue to work.

Movable tongue with 90° notch to support work

Work

Tongue pivots on ³⁄₈-in. carriage bolt.

Wedge acts against carriage bolt to hold steady rest against bed.

—17°—

2 in.

8³⁄₄ in.

10 in.

9⁷⁄₁₆ in.

Height of bed rails plus 3 in.

¹⁄₂ in.

2 in.

5⁷⁄₈ in.

Tools

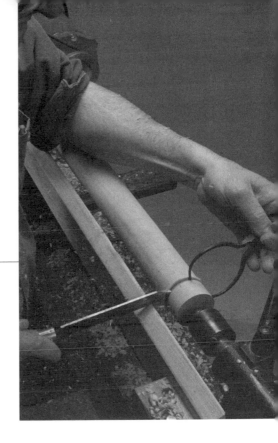

Tools are just as important to the turning process as the lathe itself. There are many varieties of tools available, ranging from splendid to abysmal. You would think that any tool offered would work fine, but this is not always the case. While the adage, "You get what you pay for," is an acceptable working axiom, some care is still necessary in the selection process.

There are three quality levels of tools: substandard, standard and premium. Substandard tools sell at a very cheap price. Little thought goes into their design or manufacture, and the steel is often inferior. Such tools are usually sold in sets and are very short in length compared with standard or premium tools.

Traditionally, turning tools were made out of high-carbon steel. Today, standard tools are still made from carbon steel. However, high-speed steel (HSS) is used in most, if not all, premium turning tools (if a tool is stamped HSS, it's more than likely premium quality). The main difference between carbon steel and HSS is that HSS stands up under heat and still maintains a sharp edge. While carbon steel tools cannot be heated above 430° F without drawing the temper, HSS tools have hot hardness, meaning they can work at high temperatures without losing their temper. Hot hardness is a result of alloying tungsten and/or large amounts of molybdenum into the steel. HSS is fairly immune from damage in the grinder due to burning and/or overheating. HSS also holds its edge longer than its carbon cousin.

Traditional

Cheap version that evolved after WWII

Modern version

Even though HSS is expensive, I recommend it for most turning tools, especially the ones that must be ground frequently (such as spindle and bowl gouges).

But the quality of steel isn't the only thing I look for in a lathe tool. It has to be the correct shape and size. That's why I shy away from sets of lathe tools. Although a tool set usually looks attractive in a mail-order catalog, it is seldom a good value. Typically a set includes a skew that is too narrow, a spindle gouge of an unneeded size, a cutoff tool that is rectangular in cross section rather than diamond-shaped, and no bowl gouge at all. A larger set will come with two or more scrapers with useless shapes (a diamond-point scraper seems obligatory), but at least these scrapers can be easily reground to useful shapes. You are much better off buying individual tools as you need them, one or two at a time, until you've built a kit.

Assembling a Lathe Tool Kit

What follows is a list of tools in the order in which I would build a lathe tool kit. I've included a drawing of each tool, showing the correct shape it should be sharpened to. This is important information because a keen edge and the correct angle are the most important factors in learning to turn and turning well thereafter (for more on sharpening, see Chapter 3). To help those on a budget, I have also indicated those tools for which carbon steel will suffice.

SPINDLE GOUGE

The first tool on my list is the spindle gouge. Modern HSS spindle gouges are milled from round bars because it is difficult to forge HSS. The result is a tool that is round in cross section (see bottom drawing at left). With the flatter gouges shown in the top drawings, the area of contact can be well to one side of the cut, causing the tool to be inherently unstable. The flatter shape also makes it impossible to grind a long fingernail profile and limits the tool's usefulness in cutting in tight places.

Because the spindle gouge is the most important tool, it is the last place to skimp. I feel that a modern HSS spindle gouge milled from round bar stock is the best. The first one to buy is a ½-in. width, with ¼ in. being the next choice. A ¾-in. spindle gouge is useful for large architectural turning but for little else. Regardless of size, the tool should be ground to a fingernail profile (see drawing, facing page).

THE SPINDLE GOUGE

Grind bevel at 30°, rolling the tool from side to side, to create a fingernail profile.

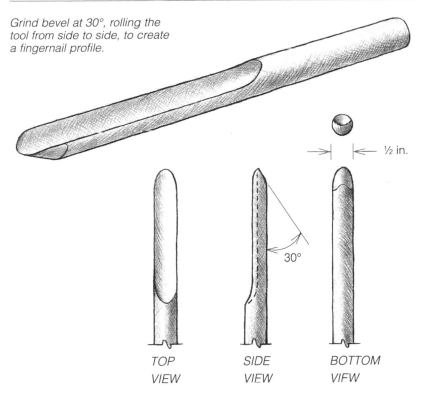

TOP VIEW   SIDE VIEW   BOTTOM VIFW

30°

½ in.

The profile of the fingernail is a matter of personal taste. I have seen turners perform equally well with a fairly blunt "working-man's" fingernail or a long "high-society" fingernail. I like the high-society grind better because the point gets into tight places, and the long sides are useful for long peeling cuts when shaping tapers and cylinders. (For more on grinding a fingernail profile, see p. 35.)

SKEW CHISEL

Your first skew should be fairly wide—1 in. or even 1¼ in. Most sets come with a ½-in. skew, which is fine in experienced hands for detail work, but this size skew is difficult for beginners to master. The larger the diameter of the work being turned, the easier it is to catch the workpiece with a skew because the corners of the chisel are closer to the surface of the work. A wider skew allows you to better see what is happening and to take corrective action *before* disaster strikes.

While all other turning tools work fine with a hollow ground bevel, the skew is the one tool that works much better with a flat bevel (to learn how to sharpen the skew, see pp. 36 and 37). The inclusive angle of grind should be about 42° (21° per side). The right amount of skewing for the edge is 15° to 20°. Makers of economy sets often skew the edge as much as 45°, and such tools do not work well. Skewing an edge to the angle of travel effectively lowers the attack angle, so a 42° grind angle yields about 30° with an average amount of skewing.

Oval skew chisels have become popular in the last few years (you can make these round with an adapter called a Stabilax). Oval skews are considerably less "catchy" than the traditional variety because the point of contact with the tool rest is brought under the area of the edge where the cut is taking place. While the round Stabilax device brings the contact point directly under the center of the cut, an oval skew only brings the contact point much closer to the cut. In either case the tendency to catch is greatly reduced. My choice would be the oval tool over the Stabilax because the latter makes a normal skew somewhat chunky and hard to get into tight spots.

THE SKEW CHISEL

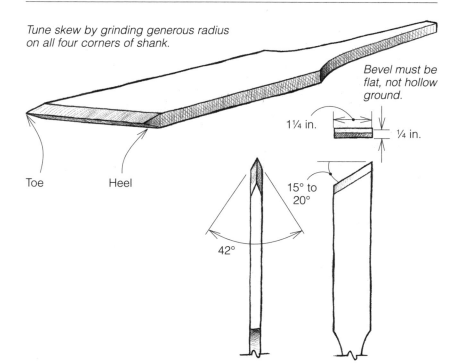

Tune skew by grinding generous radius on all four corners of shank.

Bevel must be flat, not hollow ground.

1¼ in.

¼ in.

Toe   Heel

15° to 20°

42°

Once ground to the proper bevel angle, a skew is best sharpened on a whetstone, not a grinder, so overheating while sharpening is not a problem. Which is why, if you're on a budget, a carbon-steel skew is a great way to economize on a turning kit. Many turners today grind the heel of their skew to a curved edge because of the influence of the book *Turning Wood with Richard Raffan* (Taunton Press, 1985). Richard's turning is mainly small artistic pieces with spherical shapes, not furniture parts (furniture turning is generally lumped into what is called "architectural turning"). While Richard's curved edge may be better for rounded forms, a straightedge skew, like the one shown on the facing page, is vastly superior for architectural turning. It will work up to an edge better, and the sharp toe is a more appropriate fit for detail work.

CUTOFF TOOL

The cutoff tool, also known as a parting tool, is sold in a variety of permutations. It is used to cut work away from the lathe. The three common types are economy, fluted and diamond-section cutoff tools (see drawing at right).

The economy model is a flat, rectangular section ground with two bevels at about a 50° angle that meet to form the cutting edge. This type can easily be made from an old file. The fluted cutoff tool is available only from Sorby and performs only marginally better than the third type, the diamond-section cutoff tool (which is the one I prefer). The edges of this tool are relieved, so there is less friction when working a deep kerf with this type than there is when working with the economy model. Also, the diamond-section tool can cut a narrower kerf when turning faceplate work. In this situation, the tool is parallel to the lathe bed, and the cutoff kerf is a circle.

In general, cutoff tools are available in sizes of ¹⁄₁₆ in., ⅛ in., ³⁄₁₆ in. and ¼ in. The ⅛-in. tool is a good starting size, and you can add a ¹⁄₁₆-in. model for smaller work.

ROUGHING-OUT GOUGE

The roughing-out gouge is a most useful tool to anyone turning furniture parts. Its main purpose is to bring square stock round quickly, and this it does with a vengeance. The tool is additionally useful for cutting cylinders and tapers. If well-sharpened and angled 15° to 20° to the direction of travel, it will leave almost as good a finish as a skew. Consequently, I keep mine handy and use it frequently. For this reason I put this tool in the necessary category—especially for furniture makers.

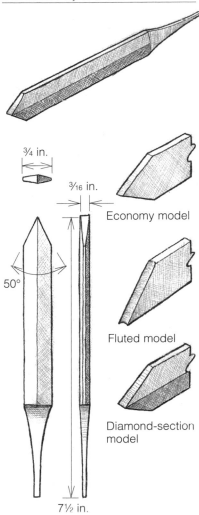

THE CUTOFF, OR PARTING, TOOL

¾ in.

³⁄₁₆ in.

Economy model

50°

Fluted model

Diamond-section model

7½ in.

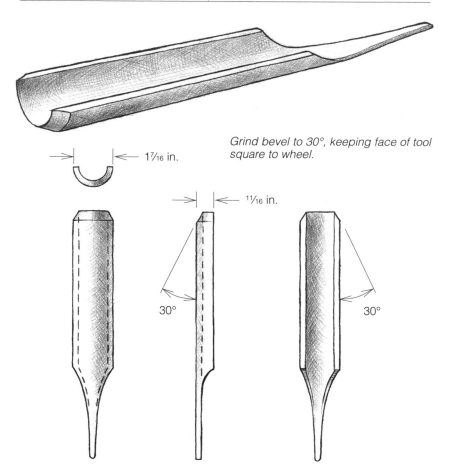

Grind bevel to 30°, keeping face of tool square to wheel.

1⁷⁄₁₆ in.

1¹⁄₁₆ in.

30°

30°

For those on a budget, this tool works well in carbon steel because it is easy to sharpen. A very large spindle gouge can sometimes be had cheaply and will make a good roughing-out gouge if the end is reground square, as shown in the drawing above. Roughing-out gouges are commonly available in widths from ¾ in. to 1½ in. For furniture making, I prefer the 1½-in. width.

SCRAPERS

A scraper is any tool that is brought to a burred edge, either through grinding and purposely leaving the burr, or through burnishing to raise a burr. (Both methods of raising a burr will be covered in Chapter 3.) While most turning "experts" rail about the evils of scraping, the truth is that there are times when scraping is the only alternative. In the 19th century, there were a good many production turners who earned decent incomes purely from serial turning of things as varied as furniture parts, shaving brushes and bottle stoppers. They did a lot of scraping, and their work survives to this day as fitting tributes to a noble profession.

Traditionally, carbon-steel scrapers were not very hard, anywhere from Rc50 to about Rc55 (Rockwell C scale). (For reference, a cabinet scraper is about Rc50.) This allowed a burr to be rolled with a burnisher. Modern HSS scrapers are well above Rc60 and are difficult to burnish by conventional means.

A turning scraper is used in a manner similar to a cabinet scraper. The burred edge is *dragged* along the work surface, with fine shavings being the result. The size of the burr limits the depth to which the tool can dig in, so a controlled chip size with limited tearout is the result. While a cabinet scraper is leaned in the direction of travel, the turning scraper is pointed downhill on the tool rest to achieve the same results. If a scraper is set level or uphill on the rest, it will catch, tearing out the wood. To prevent this from happening, always aim the tool at a generous downward slope (10° to 15°). I usually keep the tool rest a bit high for scraping cuts to ensure a dragging cut. This policy is particularly helpful for faceplate work, especially inside cuts. A scraper must be used with a very light touch in face grain. If too much pressure is applied, you will suddenly move from a highly positive shear cut by the burr to a negative-angle plow cut, which will remove the burr. When this happens, there is considerable tearout, which usually requires shear cutting with a gouge and/or extensive sanding to correct.

The drawing at right illustrates a couple of scraper shapes that I have found useful. But you don't have to buy a scraper. Almost any piece of high-grade steel can be readily ground into one, especially when only a one-time use is required. I have fashioned old screwdrivers, files and pieces of car springs into improvised scrapers, which have handled grooves, undercuts, small beads and odd shapes very well.

For most of these situations, I make what is called a form scraper. I start with a suitable piece of steel and grind it to a mirror image of the desired form (such as a small bead). An old file makes a great scraper if some care is exercised in how far it is extended beyond the tool rest. Because it may be rather brittle, it can snap in two if flexed too much. To prevent this, draw back the temper by placing the file in a kitchen oven at 450° F for an hour or so. Once the file cools back to room temperature, it will be around Rc55—and will have less of a tendency to break if flexed.

To make a form scraper, start by drawing the desired shape full-scale on a piece of paper. Then glue the drawing to the top of the piece of steel the scraper will be made from. Next grind to the shape of the drawing. A scraper needs about 15° to 20° of relief in the edge. (Grinding of form tools is also covered in Chapter 3.) The process is shown in the photos on p. 24.

SCRAPERS

RIGHT-ANGLE SCRAPER

Point is ground to 90°. Scraper is easily made from old file and is useful for chuck-making.

About ½ in. wide

DOME SCRAPER

Scrapers have 15° to 20° clearance in edge (70° to 75° inclusive grind).

About 1 in. wide

Making a Form Scraper

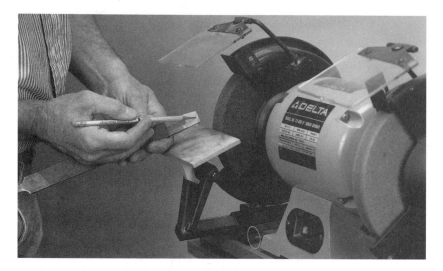

1. Draw the full-size shape on a piece of paper, then glue the drawing to the top of the scraper (in this case the form scraper is being made from an old file).

2. Next, grind to the shape of the drawing. A scraper needs about 15° to 20° of relief in the edge to work.

3. The finished scraper.

BOWL GOUGE

In furniture making, the bowl gouge is used exclusively for faceplate work (such as tabletops and stool seats). The difference between the bowl gouge and the spindle gouge is the shape of the flute. The bowl gouge has a much deeper U-shaped flute, while the spindle gouge has a shallow flute of constant radius. Depending on the manufacturer, the flute could be U-shaped or in the shape of a complex parabolic curve. This is another tool that is well worth buying in HSS.

Bowl gouges may be ground in three basic ways (see drawings below). Most furniture makers would do well to alter the typical factory grind to the modified grind. Many bowl turners grind long

THREE WAYS TO GRIND A BOWL GOUGE

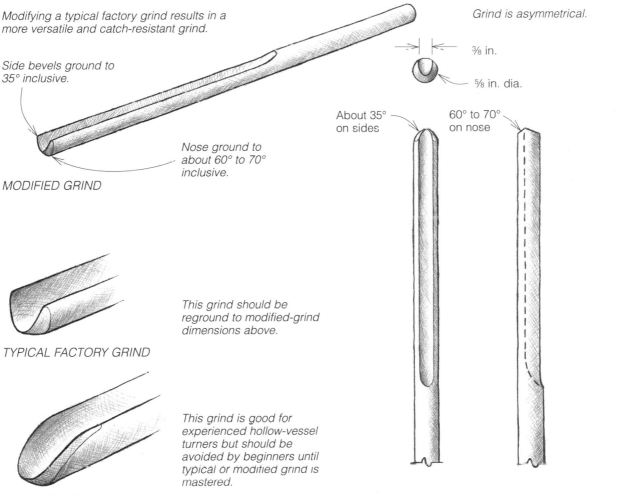

Modifying a typical factory grind results in a more versatile and catch-resistant grind.

Grind is asymmetrical.

Side bevels ground to 35° inclusive.

⅜ in.

⅝ in. dia.

Nose ground to about 60° to 70° inclusive.

About 35° on sides

60° to 70° on nose

MODIFIED GRIND

TYPICAL FACTORY GRIND

This grind should be reground to modified-grind dimensions above.

ADVANCED GRIND

This grind is good for experienced hollow-vessel turners but should be avoided by beginners until typical or modified grind is mastered.

fingernails, which I call the advanced grind. This grind can offer a more efficient turning and a better finish. The modified grind should be mastered before moving on to the advanced grind, however.

BEADING-AND-PARTING TOOL AND BEDAN

The beading-and-parting tool is just a very narrow traditional woodturners chisel. It has a double bevel ground to about 42°, but the end is square, not skewed. The bedan is simply a narrow single-bevel chisel ground to 30° (much the same as a carpenter's chisel). Both tools are offered in ⅜-in. and ¼-in. widths (see drawings below). Some turners, especially those in England, use both these tools for rolling beads, but I feel gouges are much better for this purpose.

The best use for either tool is for sizing tenons. Since a bedan is close to a normal carpenter's chisel, I have often successfully used one of my bevel-edge chisels for this purpose.

BEADING-AND-PARTING TOOL AND BEDAN

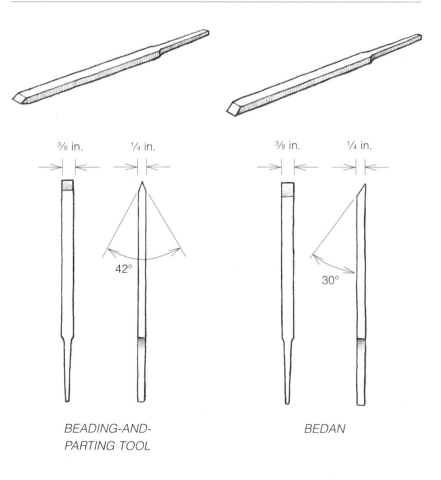

⅜ in.   ¼ in.   ⅜ in.   ¼ in.

42°   30°

BEADING-AND-   *BEDAN*
PARTING TOOL

POWER SANDER

The final tool is really not a turning tool in the strict sense, but it might as well be. It is a power sander. The best sanding method for turning I've found is a rubber sanding pad about 3 in. in diameter held in a high-speed electric drill—the faster the drill, the better. Try to find a drill that turns about 1,800 rpm or more. I use an old polishing motor that I installed a three-jaw chuck on. For speed and convenience, I like the Power Lock Pad system, which is made by Merit Abrasives.

The heart of the Power Lock Pad system is a 3-in. rubber pad mounted on an arbor that's chucked in an electric drill. This pad accepts Merit's abrasive discs, which all have a small plastic clutch glued to the back. With this system it is possible to work from 60 to 220 grit very quickly because each sanding disc simply snaps on and off the rubber pad. What is more, unexpended pads can be reused. They are not sold at every hardware store but are stocked by many specialty woodworking and wood-turning mail-order catalogs.

There are other systems on the market that use hook-and-loop fabric to hold the sanding pads to the rubber disc, but in my opinion these do not work nearly as well. The hook cloth is glued to the rubber pad, and the heat sanding generates usually does the adhesive in. There are also other clutch systems, but again I have not found these to be anywhere nearly as good as Merit's.

While power sanding is not of much use for details, it sure cleans up cylinders and tapers in short order. It will quickly remove tool marks and slight imperfections. I usually do a final sanding by hand with the grain so that all marks run in the same direction.

A rubber sanding pad mounted in a high-speed electric drill is perfect for cleaning up cylinders and tapers, quickly removing tool marks and slight imperfections.

Sharpening

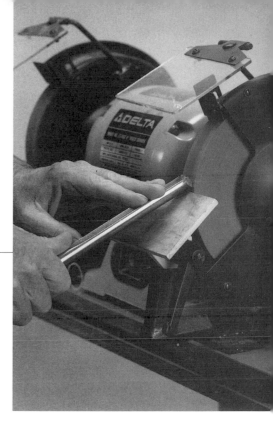

One of the most important steps to becoming proficient at wood turning is learning how to sharpen lathe tools. In my experience as a teacher, I've discovered that the main reason why people get frustrated with turning is they never start with a sharp tool. But once I place a correctly sharpened tool in the hands of a student, they take to the lathe like ducks to water.

By sharp, I mean really sharp—sharp enough to shave hair off your arm. But there's more to a turning tool than sharpness. I've had numerous students bring tools that shaved hair but did not turn wood for sour apples. The tool must also be shaped correctly and have the correct grind angles on the bevels. This can be quite a challenge, especially for a turner just starting out, because most turning tools are not delivered sharp nor with the correct grind angles. Most are not even the right shape.

For this reason, I've included drawings of each turning tool in Chapter 2. You can compare your tool to the appropriate drawing to see whether or not you have the correct grind angles. In this chapter, I'll show you how to use some basic tools and simple techniques to bring your turning tools quickly to their correct profiles.

Sharpening of lathe tools can be divided into three distinct operations: heavy grinding, light grinding and honing. Heavy grinding is necessary only when you need to establish the correct shape and bevel angle. After the correct shape is obtained, only light grinding is necessary to maintain the tool. Honing brings the ground edge really sharp.

One final thought before we jump into the sharpening process. Sharpening, like turning, is a personal thing. The methods I describe here work well for me and are based on years of turning experience. You may have a different view or have discovered a way that works best for you. I'd encourage you to experiment with different jigs and techniques. Don't fall into the "this is the only way to sharpen" trap.

The Grinder

Establishing the correct shape and bevel angle, as well as day-to-day grinding of an edge to maintain the tool, are best done with an ordinary bench grinder. Bench grinders for home up through light industrial use come in 6-, 7-, 8- and 10-in. sizes. The smaller three sizes generally use a 3,450-rpm motor, while the larger uses a 1,725-rpm motor. Although you might think the larger machine grinds cooler because of the slower speed, there is really not much difference. A 6-in. grinding wheel at 3,450 rpm has a surface speed of 5,416 ft. per

The grinder on the left is an economy grinder, which allows grinding only at 90°. The grinder on the right has an articulated rest to allow grinding at any angle. It also has metal-framed safety shields.

minute, while a 10-in. wheel running at 1,725 rpm goes 4,516 ft. per minute. Baldor sells a 6-in. grinder with a 1,725-rpm motor that gives a surface speed of 2,710 ft. per minute. While many tout the virtues of low-speed grinding, I've found there's actually a loss of efficiency at surface speeds much below 4,000 ft. per minute. There is, however, a gain in control because things happen slower. For this reason, beginners may feel more comfortable with this machine. Much more important than the speed of the grinder are other features, such as rests, safety shields, guards, lighting and wheels.

GRINDING RESTS

The grinding rest is a most important detail because it is really a jig that allows you to start grinding at the correct angle. Most grinders have a rest that is woefully inadequate for sharpening lathe tools. An economy grinder tends to have a one-piece cast-iron or aluminum rest, which must be modified to be of use to a wood turner. If you own an economy grinder with a one-piece cast rest, you can fasten a wedge of wood to the fixed rest with double-sided tape or sheet-metal screws to make it better-suited for lathe tools (top photo, right). This takes a bit of finagling to get the right angle, and you'll have to readjust it as the wheel wears. A better solution is to buy an auxiliary rest to replace the original (bottom photo, right). An auxiliary rest allows you to change angles quickly and easily and provides a larger support surface for the tool.

A one piece cast rest is easily modified so that it can be used with turning tools. Simply attach a wedge of wood to the rest with double-sided tape or sheet-metal screws.

SAFETY SHIELDS

In the past, safety shields on any grinder were metal frames with tempered safety glass in them. Sadly, most grinders today are supplied with plastic viewing shields. The fact that the mounting arm can be screwed directly to the plastic, negating the need for a metal frame, reduces manufacturing cost. If your grinder has a plastic shield in a frame, consider replacing it with a glass-plastic-glass sandwich. If done correctly, the two layers of tempered safety glass, with a sheet of plastic in between, make shattering near impossible but give a scratch-resistant surface. If you must make do with plastic, a squirt of antistatic spray from a computer shop helps reduce buildup on the shield and offers you a better view of the sharpening operation.

GUARDS AND LIGHTING

Any grinder should provide a guard that encloses the wheel except at the area just above the rest. An open, unguarded wheel is unsafe and should be avoided. Most grinders have a sliding shield called a spark arrester at the top edge of the guard. In addition to greatly reducing the sparks that could land on your hands during grinding, the spark arrester helps contain shrapnel inside the guards in case the wheel disintegrates. For best results, position the spark arrester within 1/16 in.

An auxiliary rest is easily adjustable to any angle and provides a larger support surface for the tool.

of the wheel. The tool rest should also be kept as close as possible—at least ⅛ in.—to the surface of the wheel at all times. Obviously, safety glasses are a must around any grinding equipment. If your regular glasses are not true safety types, with side shields, use goggles over them or a face shield.

Good lighting at a grinder is a must. While industrial grinders often have lighting built into the safety-shield frames, economy grinders leave lighting to the user. A simple gooseneck lamp works fine.

GRINDING WHEELS

A good practice with a new wheel, whether it is a replacement or that which came with a new grinder, is to tap it lightly with a mallet to see how it rings. As with a baseball bat, the wheel will not ring true if it is cracked. Once mounted in the grinder, stand to one side, start the machine and leave the room for a few minutes. If there is a defect in the wheel, it will usually disintegrate at, or shortly after, startup. (Never start the grinder without all guards securely in place.)

Most grinders are delivered with silicon-carbide wheels. Such general-purpose wheels are good for grinding anything from steel to glass, or even bathroom tiles. But they grind too hot for tool steel. A better choice for tool grinding is an aluminum-oxide wheel. The aluminum-oxide wheel has a bonding medium that is softer than that of the stock silicon-carbide wheel. It's important for the wheel to have the right amount of friability, which means "to crumble." Why do the wheels have to crumble? Because they are self-sharpening and self-cleaning. Old, worn particles break off, which in turn brings up fresh, sharp ones. Generally speaking, a wheel of medium friability is about right for general woodworking-tool grinding. It would also be my choice for sharpening carbon-steel tools, such as plane irons and bench chisels. Harder wheels are more aggressive and are better for initial shaping of high-speed steel (HSS) tools. Aluminum-oxide wheels can be found through mail-order woodworker catalogs.

A common mistake is to use a wheel with too fine a grit. A good roughing wheel is 46 to 60 grit, while the finishing wheel should be 80 to 120 grit. For dry grinding, never use finer than 150 grit. Bear in mind that the grit of powdered abrasives is not as coarse as hand sandpaper, which is what we generally judge abrasive grit by, because each abrasive particle penetrates less when moving at speed.

Dressing the wheels

A new wheel is about as round as a freshly mounted turning billet. It is impossible to grind well on such a wheel because the work will just hop up and down. Therefore, some means of truing your grinding wheel is as important as the grinder itself. The process of truing is referred to as dressing. It consists of making the wheel concentric with the grinding machine's arbor, squaring the face of the wheel (90° to the sides of the wheel), giving the wheel the texture desired and bringing up sharp new particles when necessary.

Several methods of dressing are available. The best method I've found to get a wheel true is to use a diamond dresser, preferably in combination with some sort of jig to ensure that the wheel is dressed round with square edges (see photo below). A diamond dresser is simply an industrial diamond brazed into the end of a piece of cold rolled steel. Setting the shank on the grinding rest and sliding the diamond tip laterally across the grinding wheel will round the wheel. The diamond dresser is optimally presented at a 5° negative (downhill) angle to the face of the wheel in a scraping cut and with a fairly light touch. (The Oneway dressing jig does this automatically.) Without a jig, you can tilt the table a bit downhill and use it to support the dresser, but it's difficult to slide it uniformly across the rest to create a surface that's 90° to the sides of the wheel.

Buying a diamond dresser is just like buying a diamond ring for a friend in that the size dictates the price. But don't worry—industrial diamonds are cheap compared to their gem-quality cousins. A good diamond dresser will cost between $15 and $60. Bigger dressers, called clusters, contain more than one diamond and cost around $60. Diamond dressers are available from mail-order catalogs and industrial tool suppliers.

The Oneway dressing jig presents the diamond dresser to the wheel at the correct 5° negative (downhill) angle and ensures that the wheel is dressed true to its axis.

An alternate way to dress a wheel is to use a star-wheel dresser, which is available at any hardware store. A star-wheel dresser follows the contour of a wheel, so it does not really make it round—only a diamond dresser can do that. However, the star-wheel dresser gives the wheel a much rougher texture than a diamond dresser, so it's great for dressing your coarse wheel (after it is made round with a diamond dresser) in preparation for initial shaping of new tools. A grinding wheel that has been dressed with a star wheel is much more aggressive than one dressed with a diamond and really removes metal fast with minimum heat. More than about two dressings with a star wheel will make the wheel out of round, and the diamond dresser will have to be brought into play again. My least favorite type of dresser is a silicon carbide stick. It is only marginally harder than the wheel and will leave a glazed surface that tends to grind hot.

As you grind, be aware that only about 10% of the surface abrasives are doing the work and quickly become dull. The area between them fills up with metal, at which time they effectively lose their clearance. When you can see steel in the surface of the wheel, when the surface looks glazed, or when the wheel has grooves worn in it, it needs to be dressed again.

QUENCHING

Quenching is the act of cooling a hot tool in water after it has been sharpened on the grinder. Quenching should not be done with HSS tools, however, because the rapid cooling will cause hairline cracks in the cutting edge. HSS tools can be brought to very high temperatures without drawing the temper, but just let them air-cool after grinding. Carbon-steel tools are another matter.

Carbon-steel tools should never be much above the boiling point of water because they will begin to lose their temper (hardness). For grinding carbon-steel tools, a good-size quenching tub should be located right next to the grinder. I use a metal tub because a hot tool can burn through the bottom of a plastic container.

Sharpening Gouges and Skews

Grinding is more a matter of practice than anything else. As mentioned earlier, a jig can greatly simplify the learning curve (for more on sharpening jigs, see Appendix B). I would call myself an accomplished tool grinder, and I cannot grind a spindle or a bowl gouge freehand as well as I can with a jig. So I always use a jig to sharpen gouges, and they can be touched up once or twice with

stones or a buffing wheel between grindings. The use of a jig
gives me the comfort of knowing that the tool will always retain
the correct profile.

If a sharpening jig is out of your economic range, or if you're just
not into jigs, then you can try sharpening freehand. If you are going to
freehand a tool, set whatever tool rest you decide to use to the
appropriate angle, turn on the grinder, set the tool on the rest, slide it
forward into the wheel and immediately start moving it laterally. This
is easy for roughing-out gouges, but for other tools, it's more difficult.

SPINDLE GOUGES

The spindle gouge is more difficult to grind than most turning tools
because it has a convex curved edge. Start with the gouge 90° to the
grinder, touching the nose to the very center of the wheel at a 30°
angle. To grind the right side of the bevel, roll the tool to the right
while simultaneously swinging the handle to the right and pushing
the tool forward and to the left (see photos below). Finish with the
tool rolled over to the right, with the bevel to the left of and higher on
the wheel than where you started. Then go back to the center of the
tool and grind the left side. Now the tool is ready for honing (for more
on honing, see pp. 37-41).

*When sharpening a spindle gouge freehand, touch the
nose of the tool to the wheel (with the table set to 30°) and
immediately start swinging the tool either to the right or
the left. In this case the author is swinging to the right.*

*As you swing the tool, simultaneously tip its handle
upward and rotate the handle slightly. The rotation is
clockwise if swinging to the right and counterclockwise if
swinging to the left. Repeat in mirror image for the other
half of the tool.*

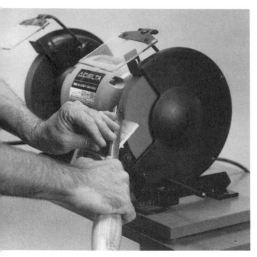

Bowl gouges are sharpened the opposite of spindle gouges. Start by laying the tool flat on the rest (set to approximately 45°) and touch the flank to the wheel.

Next, swing the handle toward center while simultaneously raising and twisting it. Repeat in mirror image for the other half of the tool.

The shape of the fingernail grind on a spindle gouge is a matter of personal preference. I like to use a long, tapered grind (what I call a "high-society" grind), but other turners prefer a blunt, "working man's" fingernail profile.

BOWL GOUGES

A bowl gouge generally has an asymmetrical grind, that is the nose has a different angle of grind from the flanks. A good general-purpose grind is shown on p. 25, with either side of the flute ground to about 35° and the nose ground to about 60° to 75°. For inside turning of deep vessels with small openings, the nose angle can be increased anywhere up to 90° as necessary. For flat, open shapes, like tabletops and stool seats, I use a smaller grind—45° on the nose and side bevels. Many bowl turners like to grind the side bevels far back on the shank of the tool, as shown in the advanced grind in the drawing on p. 25. While this has advantages for bowl turners, I don't feel it has any advantage in furniture work.

To achieve the general-purpose grind shown on p. 25, lay the tool flat on the rest (make sure the rest is set to approximately 45°) and touch the flank to the wheel. Next, swing the handle toward the center while simultaneously raising and twisting it (see photos, left). Repeat in mirror image for the other half of the bowl gouge.

Because it is difficult to raise a tool off of a flat table in the above described manner, many turners like to fabricate a rest for grinding gouges that emulates the tool rest on their lathe. There is wisdom in this idea because the movements in freehand sharpening of gouges are somewhat the same movements of actual turning. For the experienced grinder, this is the best rest for freehand sharpening of gouges, but you will have to learn to judge whether or not the bevel angle is correct.

SKEWS

Sooner or later you will hit a chuck with your skew or drop it point-first onto a concrete floor, which will necessitate a trip to the grinder. Grinding a skew presents some real problems. Most traditional skews are delivered from the factory with about a 42° angle of grind and flat bevels. All that is required to use such a tool is to hone it on a whetstone and ease the corners of the shank a bit on the grinder. As delivered, it will have very sharp corners on the shank, which dig into the tool rest. Not only will this harm the rest, but it also impedes smooth technique. By easing the corners of the shank lightly and then buffing them, the tool will slide and roll better on the rest. It will also be more pleasant to hold.

If you decide to try one of the new oval skews, they are delivered with an angle of grind that's too acute (26°), albeit flat. I have found that this grind is rather catchy, and you'll do better if the bevels are reground to a standard 42° inclusive angle. It is a simple matter to grind a flat bevel of the correct angle on any bench grinder, but the method of work will bring a cry of foul from the grinder safety people. This is because grinding a flat bevel requires grinding on the side of the wheel. If you grind on the edge of the wheel, you'll end up with a hollow grind that's not flat. All modern grinding manuals say to grind only on the periphery of the wheel. But an occasional grinding on the side of the wheel is OK if you only put light side pressure on a ½-in. or thicker wheel (the thicker, the better). Never excessively dress the side of a wheel. I usually lightly dress the sides of a wheel with a diamond dresser to true it up when I first mount it, then only dress once or twice more with a diamond during the life of the wheel.

Set the rest so that it is level (on an axis of the wheel) and use this as a place to support the shank of the tool. You will have to "guess-timate" the correct angle. As an aid, lay out a 42° angle on a piece of cardboard, cut it out and use it for comparison. When grinding on the side of the wheel, there is a tendency for the top half of the tool to be ground more than the bottom. To compensate for this, put additional pressure on the bottom half with your thumb, as shown in the top photo at right. Alternate from one bevel to the other until you form an edge and have a continuous flat.

When grinding a flat bevel for a skew on the side of the wheel, the top half of the tool tends to be ground more than the bottom. To compensate, put additional pressure on the bottom half with your thumb.

Honing

Tool steel has a natural tendency to form burrs when ground to an edge. Such a "wire" or "feather" edge rolls over during use, effectively forming a radius at the edge that cuts inefficiently. Honing leaves a polished (or near-polished) edge free of feather. There are two methods by which I hone lathe tools—buffing and whetstones.

BUFFING
I buff whenever possible because I've found it to be the fastest, most effective method. Buffing is the technique of using cloth or felt wheels, revolving at high speed and charged with abrasive compound, to improve the surface finish of metal. Many people make a buffer by simply mounting a cloth wheel in a bench grinder. But I do not feel a bench grinder makes a good buffer because it goes too fast, and the tool rest and the safety shield get in the way.

Several companies manufacture inexpensive jack shafts that are suitable for building a buffer. The shafts have a ½-in. arbor that fits readily available 6-in. diameter cloth wheels and are best powered by a ¼-hp or ⅓-hp 1,725-rpm motor (see bottom photo, right). Often a used motor can be found for a nominal price.

An inexpensive jack shaft mounted to a motor makes a simple buffer.

Mounting a buffing arbor in the lathe makes an inexpensive buffer.

Buffing wheels are categorized according to how the layers of cloth that form the wheel are sewn together. They are either spiral-sewn or cushion-sewn. As the name implies, spiral-sewn wheels are stitched in a spiral, starting at the center. Cushion-sewn wheels are stitched in concentric rings, which makes this type of wheel softer and fluffier. Spiral-sewn wheels are better for coarser compounds, where aggressive polishing action is desired, while the cushion wheels are better for final polishing, where gentle polishing action and a mirror finish is the goal.

Another way to make a small buffer is to mount a buffing wheel in the lathe itself (see photo at left). Also, small arbors with a ¼-in. or ⅜-in. shank are sold for mounting a 4-in. buffing wheel in an electric drill. You can even mount the arbor in a drill chuck in the headstock spindle of your lathe to create an inexpensive (less than $20 including the compound) and effective buffer (for more on drill chucks, see Appendix A). In the long run you may want to build a buffer to eliminate the hassle of removing the work in progress every time you need to hone a tool.

Buffing compounds

Buffing compounds are available in wax or grease and abrasive mixtures. Sold in stick form, a buffing compound is applied to the buffing wheel to "load" it with abrasives. Compounds are proprietary in formulation and are designed for use with a specific metal, although sometimes a compound will do several jobs. For instance, stainless-steel compound is good for final buffing of steel or stainless steel and works equally well on brass. For buffing lathe tools, I have found that a combination of two Dico compounds—E5 Emery and SCR Stainless—work well. Dico compounds and buffing wheels are sold in many hardware stores. E5 Emery is a fairly aggressive compound that will even remove rust from tools. It is great for initial buffing to remove grind marks. SCR Stainless is a perfect final compound to bring the surface to a high polish. It is also good for touching up a slightly dull tool between grindings. I keep a spiral-sewn wheel charged with E5 emery on the left side of my buffing arbor and a cushion-sewn wheel charged with SCR Stainless on the right side. After grinding I *lightly* buff on the left wheel, then move to the right for final finishing.

Buffing technique

While in grinding you always grind *into* the edge, with buffing you must always buff *off of* the edge. This is the major safety consideration—buffing into the edge could cause a kickback and send you to the emergency room. You must also position the surface you wish to buff tangentially to the wheel. Alternate between the bevel and the back (or flute) until all feather is removed and a polish is created at the cutting edge. Most people make the mistake of

Buffing with the tool straight into the wheel will round over the edge.

Always buff tangentially to the wheel. Alternate between the bevel and the back (or flute) until all feather is removed and the cutting edge is polished.

sticking the tool straight into the wheel, which is counterproductive (see top photo, above). The goal is to end up with a flat or slightly concave bevel leading to an edge that is free of feather. Buffing tangentially to the wheel accomplishes this (see bottom photo, above). The important thing to remember here it to use *light* pressure. Heavy buffing will round over the edge, requiring a return to the grinder.

WHETSTONES

I only resort to whetstones when absolutely necessary. The one exception to this is the skew chisel, which I always hone on whetstones. In fact, stones are the only way I sharpen a skew, unless I

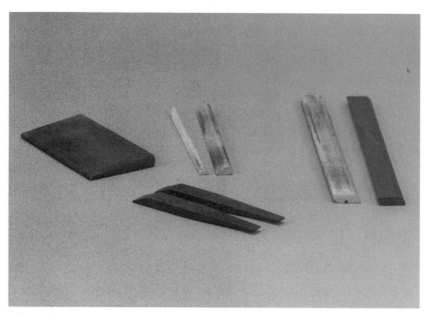

The author uses an assortment of specialty whetstones, called slips, for honing.

While honing a skew, place your hands as close to the bevel as you can get them.

nick the edge on a chuck or drop it on a concrete floor. This is because the skew is the one tool that works best with an absolutely flat bevel and a keen edge.

Whetstones are lubricated with oil or water to prevent metal particles from building up into the pores of the stone. For honing lathe tools, very fine-grit polishing stones are necessary. While I sharpen my skew chisel on the same stones that I use for plane irons and bench chisels, I have a collection of odd-shaped stones for the rest of my turning tools. These include small, tapered stones called slips and a variety of stones in triangular, round and knife-edge designs. The latter are often sold in catalogs as "files" (but they are really stones).

The trick of using a flat stone to sharpen a skew chisel is to keep the bevel absolutely flat on the stone. Again, a honing jig can be of great help here. Most of the jigs that are used for honing plane blades and bench chisels can be adapted for honing a skew. The advantage to a jig is that you will obtain a really flat bevel and a perfect edge.

If you do not have a jig, you will have to sharpen freehand. The trick here is to place the tool down on the heel of the bevel and rock forward until you *feel* the bevel go flat on the stone. Now, by locking your wrists and stroking in either a circular or back-and-forth motion, it is possible to maintain a flat, consistent angle. The proper place for your hands is as close to the bevel as you can get them, as shown in the photo at left.

To sharpen most tools, it is usually easiest to hold the tool in one hand and the stone in the other. View the operation from the side so that you can see whether the stone is contacting at the edge and the heel.

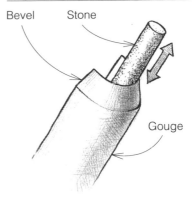

Bevel   Stone

Gouge

Hold gouge steady and move stone back and forth to remove burr on inside of gouge.

When sharpening a skew, start with a sufficiently coarse stone to remove enough metal to establish a new bevel along the entire cutting edge. (Use the same rules as if you were sharpening a chisel or plane iron.) Stop every so often and feel if you have rolled a burr along the back of the edge. The burr will be less or more pronounced, depending on the grit of the stone. Now work up to the next grade of stone and keep progressing until there is no feather edge and a polish is obtained.

For any of the other tools, it is usually easiest to hold the tool in one hand and the stone in the other. By looking sideways at the process, you can see if you have placed the stone flat on the bevel, contacting at the edge and the heel (see photo above). I often find it easier to brace the shank of the tool against the headstock or tailstock of the lathe. This gives me both leverage and steadiness. For the inside of gouges, it is just a matter of finding a stone with a radius as close to the flute radius as possible and placing it flat-side down in the flute. Now remove the burr and polish the edge with a rapid back-and-forth motion (see drawing above). I use plenty of water or oil, as required, during the entire process. Honing is much easier with hollow-ground edges because the stone will touch at the very edge and the heel of the bevel. It takes very little time to bring up a polished edge. You can usually hone several times before having to go back to the grinder.

Sharpening Scrapers

There are times in turning when a scraper is called for. The term scraper refers to a whole class of tools that are purposely sharpened to a burr and used at a downhill slant. The term scrape is misleading, however, because in reality we are taking a highly positive shear cut. The tool works exactly the same as a common cabinet scraper, and it is the burr that does the cutting. The short length of the burr effectively limits the depth of cut per revolution of the work, making it a safe, predictable tool (for more on using a scraper, see p. 23).

There are two ways to create a burr on a scraper: by grinding and burnishing (to learn how to make a form scraper, see p. 24). Grinding a scraper is simple. Set the tool rest on the grinder so that the bevel will be ground to about a 75° inclusive angle (many turners refer to this as 15° of clearance in the edge). Place the tool flat on the rest and push it into the wheel. Keeping firm pressure, swing the tool to either side to achieve the desired shape. You do not need to grind the tool upside down to achieve the burr. It forms just as well grinding right-side up, and you can see what is happening. While a ground burr works quite well, a better burr can be formed through burnishing.

Sharpening a scraper with a burnisher will only work if the tool is soft enough—it needs to be around Rc50 to Rc55 (Rockwell C scale). Normal turning tools (scrapers included) are in the range of Rc58 to Rc62. In fact, I know of no commercially available scraper soft enough to burnish with conventional methods, but it is possible to

A scraper can be made from most any piece of steel: a screwdriver, a cement nail, an Allen wrench or an old piece of spring steel.

make a scraper from a softer piece of metal and burnish it very successfully. (A burnisher is no more than a round or oval bar of very hard, polished steel.) Or you can draw the temper back in an old file. Grind the file to the desired shape and bring the area adjacent to the cutting edge to a good polish with a buffer. Carefully and evenly heat the file with a propane torch until the polished area turns a bright-blue color. Keep the torch moving all the time, and don't apply too much heat at the cutting edge. Apply more heat behind the edge so that the heat flows out to the edge. When the tip area is bright blue, quench in water. You have now drawn the temper back to about Rc50.

The burnishing process changes the crystalline structure of the steel at the cutting edge, increasing the Rockwell hardness in this area—a process called work hardening. It is not possible to burnish multiple times without first filing or grinding away this work-hardened area. After filing or grinding the bevel, a whetstone is employed to bring the bevel and the back (top surface) of the tool to a good finish. It need not be a polish, just a good finish. The burnisher is rubbed along the bevel edge with considerable force. A burr is rolled by slanting the burnisher toward the back of the tool. To get sufficient leverage, the tool must be clamped in a bench vise, and considerable body weight must be placed on the burnisher. Waxing the burnisher helps reduce friction, allowing the burnisher to slide over the metal edge easier.

Veritas Tools offers a burnishing fixture that will roll a burr even on HSS tools (see photo below). It employs a carbide cone fixed in an aluminum base, which screws to a work surface. A fulcrum pin that can be located in two positions allows levering the cutting edge of any tool against the carbide cone to roll the burr.

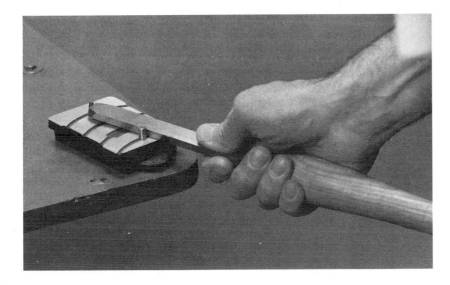

Veritas makes a burnishing fixture that will roll a burr even on HSS scrapers. Place the tool in the fixture, with the cutting edge down, and lever the cutting edge against the fulcrum pin and the carbide cone to roll the burr.

Spindle-Turning Basics

Spindles constitute the vast majority of furniture-turning work. That is not to say that faceplate work is not important in furniture making also. It's just that most of the work is done between centers. Because of this, it's important that you take the time to learn basic spindle-turning techniques. With practice, you can turn spindles quickly and efficiently, with one part looking like the previous.

The first step in turning any spindle is to prepare the stock. Your primary consideration here is the major diameter—the thickest part of the spindle. This major diameter is often repeated several times in the turning. With this in mind, you should start with a billet that is at least $\frac{1}{16}$ in. larger than the major diameter of the turning. In the case of a table leg, a portion of the turning is designed to be left square, and this dictates the size of the billet. In all furniture work, exact centering of billets is paramount. I've found that a steel ruler is an effective way to find center. The intersection of two lines connecting the corners is the place to mark, square or not. I always center-punch the intersection lightly because it makes chucking easier. There are a number of jigs (the simplest of which is a center finder that attaches to better combination squares, such as those made by Starrett) on the market to find centers quickly. But one end or the other of a billet is often not quite square, which will throw any jig off. Fortunately, this slight amount of unsquareness in no way affects the final turning.

With the centers marked on the billet, it can be chucked in the lathe and brought round with a roughing-out gouge. With a bit of practice, you can develop a feel for round since the cutting of the tool smooths as the cut becomes continuous rather than interrupted. A trick for checking for round without shutting off the lathe is to touch the spinning work lightly with the bottom side of the tool. If the work is not round, you'll hear a click-click-click sound. But the way I prefer to check is to cradle the spinning billet *lightly* in the palm of my hand to feel whether the billet is round or not. After the billet is just round, cut a bit sideways with the roughing-out gouge in a light planing cut, or bring a 1-in. or wider skew into play. The result is a smooth, consistent major diameter.

Shear Cutting and Scraping

Shear cutting leaves a smooth surface with crisp definition in need of little sanding (see drawing below). A correctly sharpened roughing-out gouge is the simplest turning tool to shear-cut with (see left photo, facing page). Simply present the tool to the work at too high an angle to cut, then raise the handle until the tool starts to cut. You now have the bevel rubbing on the work, with the highest-angle shear cut the grind of the tool will allow. Slide the tool sidewise on the tool rest for roughing out and angle it to the left or right for final turning of cylinders and tapers before moving on to other tools. Shear cutting

SHEAR CUTTING WITH A GOUGE

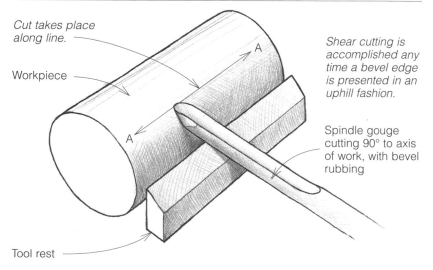

Cut takes place along line.

Workpiece

A

A

Tool rest

Shear cutting is accomplished any time a bevel edge is presented in an uphill fashion.

Spindle gouge cutting 90° to axis of work, with bevel rubbing

Present the roughing-out gouge to the work at too high an angle to cut, then raise the handle until the tool starts to cut. With the bevel rubbing on the work, slide the tool sideways on the rest for roughing out, and angle it to the left or right for final turning of cylinders and tapers.

Shear cutting with the spindle gouge uses the same technique as with the roughing-out gouge. Cut in the center of the fingernail with the bevel rubbing and slide the tool sideways on the rest.

To make a shear cut with the skew, place the corner of the shank on the tool rest, and place the heel of the bevel on the work. Tip the tool downward onto the bevel until it just starts to cut.

with the spindle gouge uses the same technique as the roughing-out gouge (see middle photo, above). But where the spindle gouge really excels is in rolling coves and beads, which is explained on pp. 48-51.

I use the shear-cutting technique with most other tools as well, not just the roughing-out and spindle gouges. One of the toughest tools to master is the skew. But if used properly, the results are fast and magnificent—the tool can even be fun. Place the corner of the shank on the tool rest, and place the heel of the bevel on the work, as shown in the right photo above. Tip the tool downward onto the bevel until it just starts to cut. Normal cutting should take place near the heel of the skew, as shown in the drawing on p. 48. As you approach a shoulder, slide the tool forward on the rest so that cutting takes place on the very heel. Cutting in the proximity of the toe will usually result in a catch, which will damage the piece.

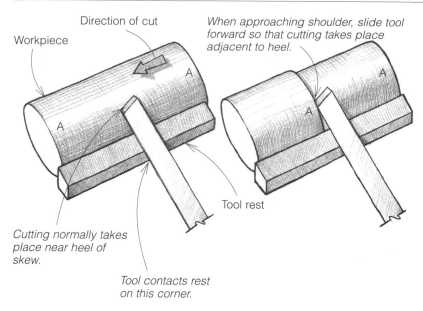

Workpiece

Direction of cut

When approaching shoulder, slide tool forward so that cutting takes place adjacent to heel.

A

A

A

Tool rest

Cutting normally takes place near heel of skew.

Tool contacts rest on this corner.

When shear cutting with the cutoff tool, place the edge of the tool on the rest and present it at too high an angle to cut. Then slowly raise the handle until the tool begins the cut.

When shear cutting with the cutoff tool, place the edge of the tool on the rest and present it at too high an angle to cut. Then slowly raise the handle of the tool until it cuts (see photo at left). If you're cutting large diameters, the friction of the tool on the sides of the kerf can become a problem. As the work is about to be parted off, cradle the cutoff portion loosely in your hand and grab it as it falls away. I try to plan cutoffs near the headstock end on larger furniture parts because the driving force to the part is removed by the cutoff.

Cutting Coves and Beads

I use a shear cut to shape coves and beads, too. Most spindle-turning shapes encompass the turning of either the cove or the bead, and mastering these two shapes will allow you to turn just about anything. A good starting place is the cove, which is best cut with the gouge. It is necessary to obey the law of perpendiculars during the cutting of any coves or beads, as shown in the top drawing on the facing page.

The idea is to start at the top edges of the cove and take a series of scooping cuts, always ending at the exact bottom. To obey the law of perpendiculars, the gouge must be rolled as the cut progresses. It starts almost on its side and ends up at the bottom dead level. Most beginners try to lock the handle into their side and simply roll the tool to scoop out the bead, which always results in a catch. When cutting a compound shape, you cannot simply roll the tool because you must keep the bevel rubbing. That's why, in addition to rolling, the tool must be angled left or right and slid slightly forward to keep the bevel rubbing. The drawing below shows this more clearly. Note the amount of handle movement required.

The most common mistakes in cutting a cove are failure to roll the gouge sufficiently at the start (it should almost be on its side) and failure to angle the tool left or right sufficiently to have the bevel rubbing at the start of the cut. You need to compensate like this because the diameter is getting smaller, and the tangent point to the surface is moving away from the tool rest.

THE LAW OF PERPENDICULARS

Perpendicular drawn from spindle gouge should coincide with perpendicular drawn from surface of work.

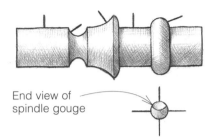

End view of spindle gouge

CUTTING A COVE WITH A GOUGE

1. Start with spindle gouge almost on its side.

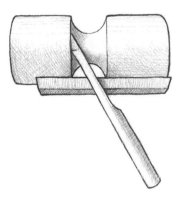

2. Move gouge in scooping action while simultaneously rolling it left and moving it forward slightly.

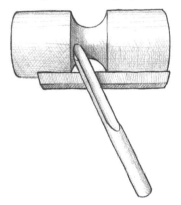

3. Finish at bottom of cove with gouge horizontal.

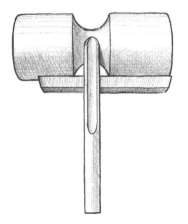

4. Repeat procedure from opposite side.

Another common mistake is to try and cut a cove with too large a gouge. To provide sufficient cutting clearance, the cove *must* be wider than the gouge. Therefore, a range of spindle gouges for cutting different-size coves is useful. I try to use a gouge that is about three-fourths the size of the cove I plan to cut.

The bead requires almost the opposite actions of the cove. The difference is that it may be cut with either the gouge or a chisel (skew, bedan or beading-and-parting tool). Although it is fun to cut beads with the skew, the gouge is much better suited to the purpose. While the process is straightforward and simple with the gouge, it requires a precise sense of being flat on the bevel with any of the chisels.

The first task in cutting a bead is laying it out. Just draw two pencil lines to mark the width of the bead. Then proceed to cut it directly into the surface of a cylinder. At first you may find it easier to use the toe of a skew chisel to define the limits of the bead. I even encourage students to cut away on either side to leave a raised square ridge, properly called a rondel. You may now cut your bead without the worry of the bottom edge of the gouge catching on the adjoining surfaces.

Whether you are starting with a rondel or cutting directly into the surface of a cylinder, start in the middle of the bead in a shear cut (see drawing, facing page). Then angle the tool left, slide it back slightly on the tool rest and roll it in the direction of the cut. Raise the handle as the cut progresses, and you should end up with the tool aimed at the center of the work. (The tool axis is now aligned with a radius of the work.) Push forward until you reach the bottom of the bead while simultaneously bringing the handle around to create the curve of the bead and keep the bevel rubbing. I realize this sounds complex, but with a little practice, it will become second nature.

If you are cutting into the surface directly, you will have to reverse the gouge and open up the area adjacent to the bead slightly. This actually entails cutting half a bead from the other direction. Many turners fail to lift the handle sufficiently and roll the tool exactly on its side at the final stage of the cut. They try to end the cut with the tool rolled 45° and the handle raised only slightly. The result is a catch by the lower flank of the fingernail on the adjoining surfaces. Making both halves of a bead symmetrical will come with practice. The nice thing about using a gouge is that you can fine-tune a bead by recutting it by halves. While this can also be done with a skew, it is more difficult, and a catch is much more likely.

It's common for turners to use the toe of a skew to incise a small groove—called a bevel—at each edge of the bead where it meets the cylinder. On most furniture turnings, this entails only a light scribing cut with the toe of a skew, while on larger architectural turnings a definite groove is incised with intersecting cuts by the toe of a skew. This simple technique deepens the bead and sets it off as an interesting accent.

NORMAL VIEW (STANDING AT THE LATHE)

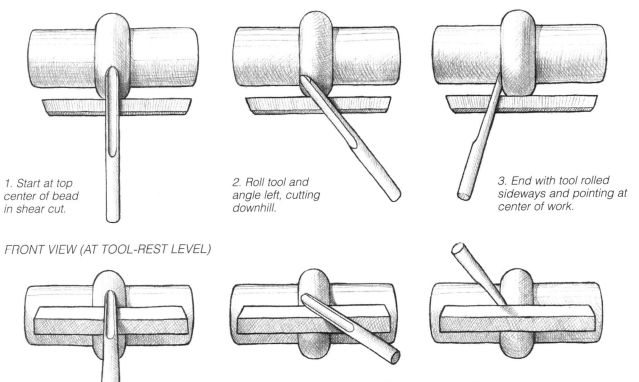

1. Start at top center of bead in shear cut.

2. Roll tool and angle left, cutting downhill.

3. End with tool rolled sideways and pointing at center of work.

FRONT VIEW (AT TOOL-REST LEVEL)

Note large up-and-down handle movements not apparent in normal view.

Duplication

Another important aspect of turning for a furniture maker is duplication, for how well the turned elements in a table or chair match says a good deal about the craftsmanship of the entire piece. Most people believe that alike means to the nearest $\frac{1}{1000}$ in. Well, we are building furniture here, not watches. Wood movement from changes in humidity in the order of $\frac{1}{8}$ in. is not impossible. The goal is to make each piece nearly alike, not exactly alike. Plus or minus $\frac{1}{16}$ in. is a good tolerance to work for in most furniture-turning situations. This means that no two pieces can vary from each other more than $\frac{1}{8}$ in. total. While one would think that having the diameters match is more important, having each element of the turning at the same height from the floor (or same distance from one end) is actually a more critical factor.

A master part provides a tangible reference for adjusting calipers and dividers, and it serves as the visual informant for turning further parts.

MASTER PARTS AND PATTERN STICKS

Before you can duplicate a part, you must be able to visualize it. A master part or a pattern stick will help ensure that each element is placed at an exact distance from one end of the turning. A master part is the simplest and quickest method when a small number of turnings is required. This is usually the case when making one or two pieces of furniture.

Once you have an acceptable master part, it becomes the basis of all further parts. What I've found works best is to place this behind the lathe as you are turning. The master part then is available for adjusting calipers and dividers to critical dimensions and distances, as well as a visual reference to create the same shape. Transferring the elements from the master part to the turning you are working on can be handled in a variety of ways. If you are using a tool rest that is longer than the turning, the easiest option is to put masking tape on the rest and draw lines at the critical points. This makes putting the elements in their proper place quick and easy. If the tool rest is shorter than the turning and so has to be moved, then one must revert to rulers and dividers. This is one of the few instances that I like a tape measure, for it can be hooked over the end of the master part or the actual turning and leaves your other hand free for marking. Dividers are great for stepping off the length of tenons and the width of coves and beads. I've found it's best to measure with a tape to one edge of coves and beads, then set their sizes with a set of dividers.

Master parts are fine for duplicating one or two parts, but a pattern stick is my choice for long productions runs, especially if the part in question is for a piece of furniture that you will be making periodically (see photos below). To make a pattern stick, simply draw

To make a pattern stick, draw the part full-size on a thin strip of wood the same width of the billet from which you will turn the part.

Transfer the lines from the pattern stick to the rounded billet.

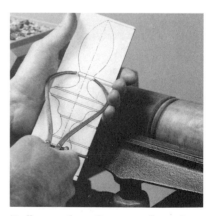

Pull secondary diameters from the pattern stick using calipers.

out the part in question full-size on a thin strip of wood. The wood strip should be the same width as the billet from which you will turn the part. The pattern stick then gives you all the information you need to turn the part, from sawing the correct-size billets to getting each element the correct size and in the correct place. While some workers only draw half the spindle, I like to draw the entire piece, which makes setting calipers at critical dimensions easier. With a half pattern, you have to measure, double the results and set the calipers with a ruler. Perpendiculars are drawn at critical dimensions, and notches are cut or sawn where they intersect the edge of the strip. This allows you to hold the pattern stick up to the spinning work and transfer these critical points to the work by placing a pencil in the notches. I like to set the pattern stick at a suitable viewing point because it is also a visual reference, just as a master part is.

MATCHING DIAMETERS

The second most important factor in duplication is to get all of the diameters as close to each other as possible. As stated previously, plus or minus ¹⁄₁₆ in. is a good rule of thumb for most situations. Obviously, a very small turning would require a much tighter tolerance on the order of plus or minus ¹⁄₃₂ in., or even ¹⁄₆₄ in., while an 8-ft. column that was 12 in. in diameter at the base could stand a lot more variance. Plus or minus ¼ in. would probably not be noticed.

There are a number of aids that can be employed in sizing spindles. The best of these are calipers (see photo, right). One can never have enough calipers, so I'm always on the lookout for them at flea markets. It is nice to have a pair for each diameter you plan to size. The calipers are used in combination with a cutoff tool.

Use the tool in the usual way at the point you want to size with the calipers. As you approach the diameter, lightly touch the calipers down in the kerf made by the tool. As the exact size is reached, the calipers will drop over the spindle, and you know to stop cutting. There is a natural tendency to force the calipers a bit, and they have enough spring to pop over the spindle when it is still considerably oversize. A light touch will ensure that they drop over, rather than pop over, the spindle. The kerf you have just created now acts as an indicator as you complete the turning. Simply turn down to this point in the natural act of completing the spindle. By placing such indicators at regular distances along a taper, it is possible to reproduce the taper time and again. This is especially important with tapers on larger legs or architectural work such as columns.

The calipers should be used with a light touch, and a firm grip should be kept on them at all times. If they bind in the kerf, they can be thrown with considerable force. For this reason I keep my face to

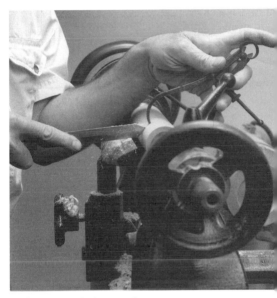

Calipers can help you determine an exact diameter easily.

the left of this operation, so the calipers will go by me if things go awry. To lessen the likelihood of binds, it's important to use a cutoff tool that is at least one-and-a-half times wider than the calipers.

A turner's gate is a device akin to calipers (see drawing below). It is meant to go on a wide cutoff tool or a bedan and allows consistent sizing of a specific diameter. The tool is fussy to set because you loosen set screws or knobs that hold it to the chisel and move it along the shank. The gate must be removed each time the tool is sharpened, and the entire setup repeated. Although the tool is started normally in a shear cut, you must allow the tool to ride down into a scrape cut for the gate to work. I don't use these much, but they are useful if are doing a large production run, where an exact size is needed. A chairmaker who is constantly sizing tenons may find it useful. In this instance the gate would best be mounted on a bedan so that the tenon could be sized in one pass.

The method I prefer to size a tenon is with an open-end wrench (see photo, facing page). I keep an inexpensive set at the lathe just for this purpose. There are two reason why I like to use them. First, they match the incremental sizes of most tenons—there's no adjustments to make. Second, open-end wrenches are slightly oversize—that is, a

A TURNER'S GATE

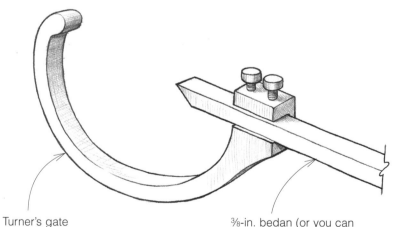

Turner's gate

⅜-in. bedan (or you can use a cutoff tool)

½-in. wrench is slightly larger (1/64 in.) than ½ in., so it will slip easily over a nut or bolt. This extra clearance will produce a tenon that will ensure a tight fit in a round mortise.

The final aid in duplication that I would like to mention is what I call seeing the big picture. Many turners will concentrate on where the tool is touching the work, and little else. As confidence is gained, it is necessary to simultaneously view the outline of the spindle as well. By looking tangentially at the top edge of the work, you will see its shape clearly, just as if you were looking at a mechanical drawing of that half of the spindle. For some people, throwing their eyes slightly out of focus helps in this process. This is also part of reading the "ghost." That is, seeing the outline of the billet when it is not yet square. The corners are hard to discern, but looking closely with the proper lighting will allow you to see the ghost. Seeing the ghost is paramount for turning from square to round at the terminus of the pommel on table legs, turning cabriole legs or any time a portion of a turning must be left square.

An open-end wrench is a tool that makes it easy to size tenons.

Part Two

TURNING FURNITURE PARTS

Table Legs

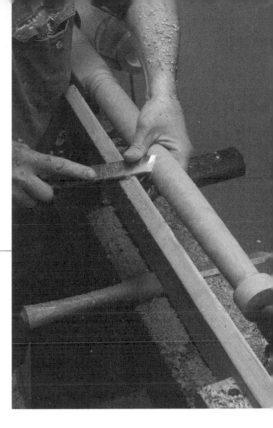

Since a table leg is a common first turning project, it is a natural place to start our exploration of furniture parts. There are many styles of turned table legs from which to choose, ranging from simple tapers to those that are highly ornate. Most leg styles are turned between centers using a single set of center points to position the leg on the lathe. This simple mode of spindle turning is called single-axis turning. Other, more sculpted legs, such as cabriole, are created by mounting off the original center points and turning on a new axis (called multiple-axes turning). Since much of the technique is similar for both methods, let's start with simple, single-axis turning.

As you're probably going to turn more than one leg, duplication is easier when you start with carefully dimensioned stock. Each billet should be straight, perfectly square and free of knots or defects. I generally cut an extra billet in case of a mishap (it also allows for some experimentation during the turning).

After the billets are cut to size, the next step is to consider joinery. If mortises are to be cut in the pommel (square portion) of the leg, as in the drawing on p. 58, I add 1 in. to the length of the billet. This extra inch helps prevent the pommel from splitting during mortising and can be trimmed off before assembly. Mortising can be carried out before or after turning. Many turners prefer to do it afterward so that the time spent cutting the mortises isn't wasted if the turning

MORTISED TABLE LEGS

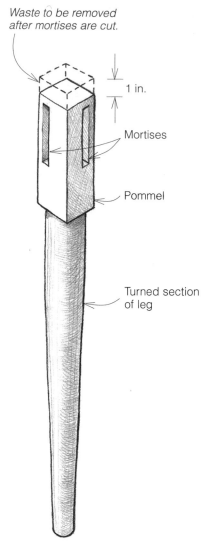

Waste to be removed after mortises are cut.

1 in.

Mortises

Pommel

Turned section of leg

is unsuccessful. But as confidence is gained, you may want to cut them before they're turned—the square billet is easier to clamp and hold for mortising.

Now you can lay out exact centers by drawing diagonals from the corners and marking out the bottom of the pommel (if there is one). You do not need to draw a line all the way around the billet to mark the bottom of the pommel—just a dark line on one flat will do. Once the lathe is started, you will be able to see the single line on one flat as a continuous line around the billet. This is a result of a phenomenon called persistence of vision, which makes motion pictures possible.

Turning Single-Axis Legs

If you're turning a round leg without a pommel, it's a simple matter of turning the billet round and then adding the details. But since most legs require a pommel for joinery, you're faced with the challenge of turning from square to round. To avoid splitting the corners of the pommel, precise turning is necessary. It's not a difficult technique; it just takes some practice to gain confidence.

Turning square to round can be accomplished with either a skew chisel or a spindle gouge. I've found beginners have the best luck using a skew. The trick is to use only the very toe of a well-sharpened skew chisel and to present the tool with the toe down, the cutting edge absolutely vertical, and the toe exactly on the centerline. Because most spindle turning is carried out with the tool rest a bit above the centerline, this generally puts the tool sloping downhill a bit. Moderate (1,100 rpm) to high (1,700 rpm) speed helps ensure a smooth cut.

CUTTING A SHOULDER

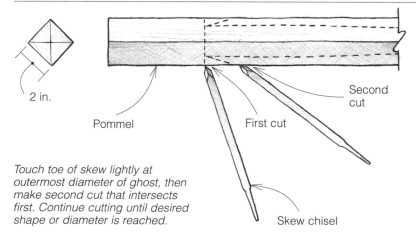

2 in.

Pommel

First cut

Second cut

Skew chisel

Touch toe of skew lightly at outermost diameter of ghost, then make second cut that intersects first. Continue cutting until desired shape or diameter is reached.

When the lathe is running, a faint pattern of the work is created by the corners of the spinning billet. This pattern is called the ghost. (Sufficient speed and a bright light will help distinguish the ghost.) Use the ghost as a reference to create a shoulder at the bottom of the pommel (see bottom drawing, facing page). The trick is to touch the toe of the skew lightly at the outermost diameter of the ghost, then make a second light cut from the side that intersects the first (see photo at right). The process is similar to chopping a log in half with an ax. These cuts must always be wide enough so that the bevel is not crowded against the shoulder, which could split the work.

continued on p. 62

Read the ghost carefully and place the toe of the skew at a high angle, with the corner rubbing. Then raise the handle until it starts to cut.

TURNED LEG SHAPES

All legs turned from 2-in. stock but projected at 45°.

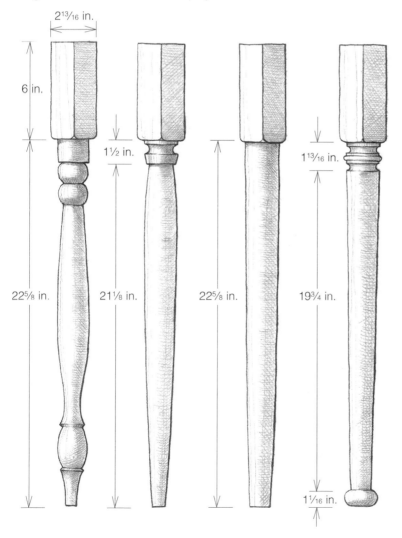

Turning a Single-Axis Leg

1. *Mount a square billet between centers. A light rap with a mallet will ensure that the drive center seats properly.*

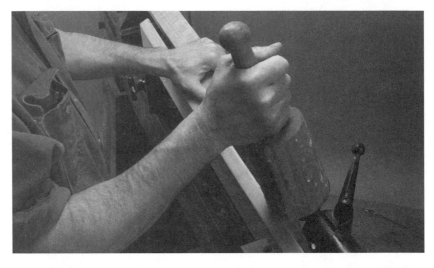

2. *After cutting the shoulder of the pommel with a skew (see p. 58), bring the rest of the leg round using a roughing gouge. Be careful near the shoulder, and don't be afraid to use a spindle gouge to clean up the last inch. The resulting cylinder should yield the major diameter of the leg.*

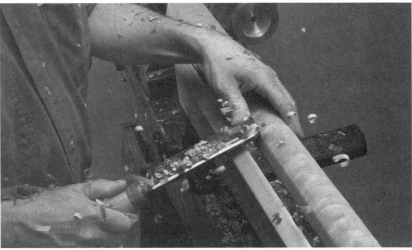

3. *Lay out the elements of the leg using a pattern stick, a ruler or a drawing.*

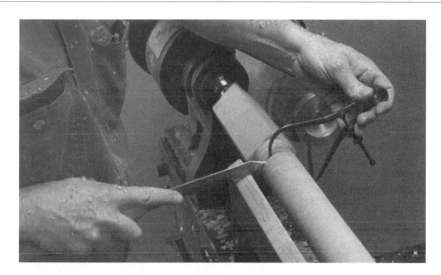

4. Use calipers in combination with a cutoff tool to size minor and critical intermediate diameters.

5. With critical and intermediate diameters sized, turn the details of the leg. Here the author cuts a bead with the spindle gouge.

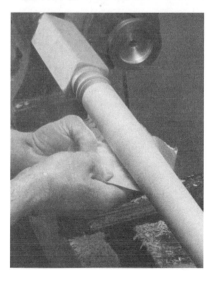

6. If you've used very sharp tools and shear-cutting techniques, very little sanding is necessary.

Once the shoulder is created, it can be left square, or you can cut a convex or concave transition with a spindle gouge. What you choose depends on the leg design. A convex or concave transition entails cutting either a bead or a cove over the corners of the newly created shoulder at the bottom of the pommel. For this cut to be successful, you'll need to keep the lathe moving at moderate to high speed and pay close attention to the ghost. It's also important to adhere strictly to the law of perpendiculars (see p. 49) and use the gouge dead on the bevel in a shear cut. Before commencing the actual bead or cove, just place the tool at a high angle, then raise the handle until it just starts to cut. It's my experience that a series of light cuts produces a crisper, cleaner detail (with less chance of a mishap) than a single, heavy cut.

After the transition from the pommel is made, the remainder of the leg can be turned round (a roughing-out gouge makes quick work of this). Once round, it is just a matter of creating the shape desired. Table legs are often long and thin enough that a steady rest is necessary. Not only does turning go much faster with a steady rest (because you can take heavier cuts), but the extra support means less chatter and a smoother surface. As with all spindle turning, it is important to work from the center of the piece to the ends, doing the thinnest sections last. The photos on pp. 60 and 61 should help you visualize the process.

Turning Multiple-Axes Legs

Once you're comfortable with single-axis turning, you can explore the challenges of multiple-axes turning—the variations are limitless. One of the most common applications of multiple-axes turning in furniture construction is a turned cabriole leg. While true cabriole legs incorporate an S-curve and are sculpted, it is possible to turn cabriole-like legs. Although sculpted cabriole legs are not exclusive to Queen Anne furniture (the ancient Egyptians used the leg style in their pieces), turned cabriole legs are. Such turned legs first appeared during the Queen Anne period and were often put at the back of case pieces to reduce production costs—labor-intensive sculpted legs were saved for the front of the pieces.

Most turned cabriole legs are of the converging-axes type, which are created by offsetting the top and bottom of the leg in *opposite* directions to create a new axis that *intersects* the old axis about 1/8 in. below the bottom of the pommel. Another leg style is the parallel-axes type, in which both ends of the leg are offset in the same direction so that the new axis is *parallel* to the original. The disadvantage to this method is that much larger turning squares are necessary to obtain the same result as a converging-axes leg. Parallel-axes cabriole legs are used extensively on chairs, the most well-known example of which is a chair unique to the Dutch settlers of the Hudson River Valley. Properly called a Hudson River Valley Chair, it is often referred to as a "duck-footed" chair. In both cases, the leg is created by first turning the foot between centers, then offsetting the billet to a new axis to create the tapered shaft and the top of the foot.

CONVERGING-AXES LEGS

One of the trickiest parts to turning a converging-axes cabriole leg is figuring the proper center offsets, which must be precise and in *opposite* directions across the diagonals at the ends of the billet. The best course of action is to carefully draw the leg full-size and then measure the offsets. This does not require sophisticated drafting skills and can be done at the work bench with a 36-in. steel ruler. I often use

CONVERGING-AXES CABRIOLE LEG

STEP 1
Draw leg full-size. Then determine first axis and locate ankle height.

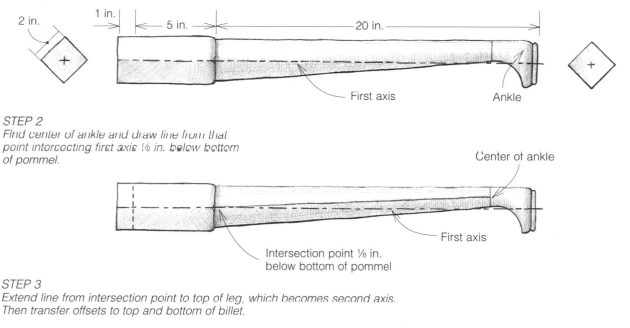

2 in.

1 in.

5 in.

20 in.

First axis

Ankle

STEP 2
Find center of ankle and draw line from that point intersecting first axis ⅛ in. below bottom of pommel.

Center of ankle

First axis

Intersection point ⅛ in. below bottom of pommel

STEP 3
Extend line from intersection point to top of leg, which becomes second axis. Then transfer offsets to top and bottom of billet.

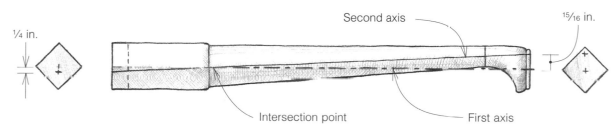

Second axis

¹⁵⁄₁₆ in.

¼ in.

Intersection point

First axis

shelf paper for such work because it is more than wide enough and can be unrolled to almost any length. The drawing, with offsets indicated, can then be glued to a thin strip of plywood to become a pattern stick.

The critical factors in figuring the offsets are the ankle diameter and its height above the floor and the location of the bottom of the pommel (if mortises are to be cut, add an inch of waste to the height of the pommel, which will be removed after mortising).

After you've drawn the leg full size, draw the first axis, which is the center of the billet. Next, locate the height of the ankle and then find the ankle's center. Draw the second axis from that center point so that

Turning Wood Pins for Mortise-and-Tenon Joints

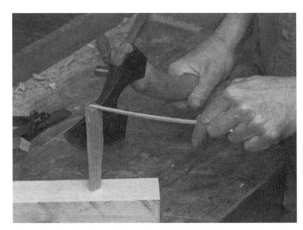

1. Split out billets large enough to obtain ¼-in. squares. Only two sides need to be split.

2. True up the sides with a hand plane.

One of the strongest, most common ways to join furniture parts together is with a mortise-and-tenon joint. For added strength, a cross-hole is drilled through the joint, and a tapered wooden pin is driven in to "lock" the pieces in place. While most furniture joints rely on glue to hold them together, pinning ensures the joint will stay tight, even if the glue fails. The problem with pinning a joint is finding a dowel to match the wood used for the project. You can use a contrasting wood as an accent, but I prefer to turn my own pins from the same wood. This way the pin is virtually invisible, and the taper creates a tighter fit.

For a pinned joint, it is important that the tenon be sufficiently long so that the wood cannot break out behind the cross-hole. The cross-holes must also be far enough from the edge of the leg (usually between ⅛ in. and ¼ in.).

A common pin diameter for furniture work is ¼ in. Historically, the tapered pin was whittled from a split billet, which ensures that all of the grain fibers are parallel. This yields a consistently stronger pin than that which is made from a sawn billet.

it intersects the first axis ⅛ in. below the bottom of the pommel. Extend this line to the top of the leg to find the offset center points at the top and bottom of the leg (see drawings on p. 63).

Once you've laid out and marked all the centers on the billet and have marked the bottom of the pommel with a single line on one flat, you can begin turning the leg. First punch all center points to make mounting much simpler and more accurate.

Mount the billet on the true center points and turn the bottom of the pommel and the foot and pad. Note: If your offset is large, and the second-axis center point is near the edge of the billet, you may need to turn the shaft first. If you turn the foot and the pad first, it's possible

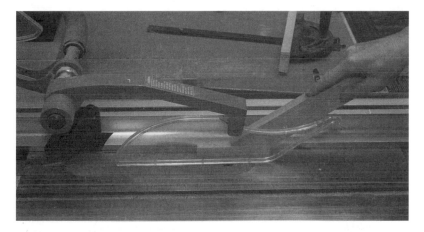

3. Trim the billet to ¼ in. on the table saw, placing only the planed sides against the fence. Cut to a suitable length (about ¼-in. longer than the size of the pommel).

4. Chuck the billet in a four-jaw chuck or, lacking a chuck, between centers and turn just round. Then use a skew to turn a slight taper.

5. Cross-drill the joint, tap the pin home and trim off the excess.

to remove the offset turning point as you create the pad. It's not necessary to turn the bottom of the pommel at this point (there are many antique examples where bottoms were turned after offsetting). This makes the radius of each corner of the pommel above the bottom uneven, but the shaft will connect to the pommel perfectly.

Once the foot and pad are turned, offset to the new axis. When the lathe is started, the shaft, ankle and top of the foot will be readily apparent as a ghost. It is now just a matter of turning to this ghost.

Turning a Converging-Axes Leg

1. Lay out the true and offset center points. Then punch them to make mounting easier and more accurate.

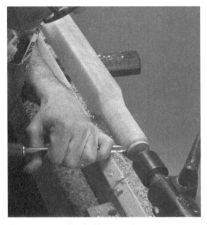

2. Mount the billet on the true center points, turn the bottom of the pommel and then the foot and pad.

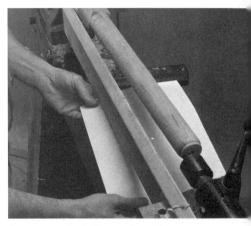

3. Mount the billet on the offset centers (the second axis). Holding a sheet of paper behind the spinning billet will help you see the ghost.

5. Finish turning the top of the foot with a ½-in. spindle gouge. Place the gouge high and raise the handle until it cuts, then cut a cove to form the top of the foot.

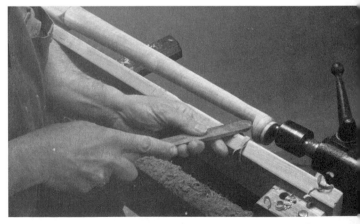

6. In a friendly wood, such as mahogany, cove the top of the foot with a round-nose scraper held downhill in a true scraping cut.

Rough in the top of the foot by cutting a large, gentle cove with a ½-in. spindle gouge. Start well above the actual foot and establish the ankle diameter. Then use a roughing-out gouge to turn the shaft between the rough cove and the bottom of the pommel. (If you are turning the bottom after offsetting, it would be turned before this operation.)

Next, finish turning the top of the foot with a ½-in. spindle gouge. Pay particular attention to the ghost, place the gouge carefully and obey the law of perpendiculars. Begin the cut by placing the gouge

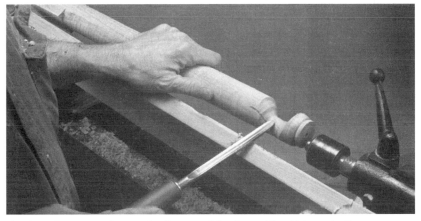

4. Cut a large, gentle cove in the top of the foot with a ½-in. spindle gouge. Start well above the actual foot to establish the ankle diameter. Then remove the remainder of the waste on the shaft by turning a gradual taper.

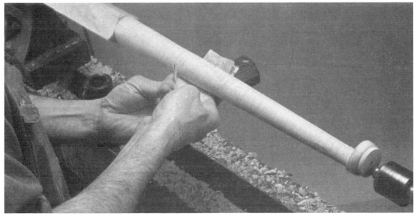

7. Sand the shaft and the top of the foot while offset, then remount the leg on the true centers to sand the bottom of the foot and the pad.

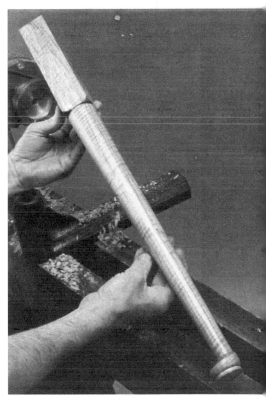

8. The finished leg.

high and raising the handle until it just cuts, then form the top of the foot with the cove cut. (In a friendly wood, such as mahogany, the above operation can be done with a round-nose scraper sharpened to a burr and held downhill in a true scraping cut.)

With the leg shaped, sand the shaft and the top of the foot, then reset to the true centers to sand the bottom of the foot and the pad. Use a quarter sheet of sandpaper so that your fingers won't be pulled into the work should the paper get caught. After sanding, but before assembly of the piece, I apply a finish. The advantage to this is that the legs can be remounted easily to sand between coats of finish (the photos on pp. 66 and 67 illustrate the process).

PARALLEL-AXES LEGS

A parallel-axes leg has a vertical shaft, as opposed to the converging-axes shaft, which tapers inward from the offset center. Figuring the offset for parallel axes legs is a bit simpler, as you only need to know the ankle diameter (see drawing below). Start with a billet that's oversize by the amount the foot will project. Lay out the true center points (the first axis), then mark the foot center points (the second axis). Then bandsaw the excess wood off at the top of the leg rather than turning it.

Mount the billet in the lathe on the second axis and turn the pommel and the foot. Remount on the first axis and turn the shaft and ankle. Particular care should be taken when turning the top of the foot, which is an interrupted cove cut. While friendly woods like mahogany can be scraped, most other woods will do best by shear cutting. Then simply finish detailing the leg, sand, stain and finish it.

PARALLEL-AXES CABRIOLE LEG

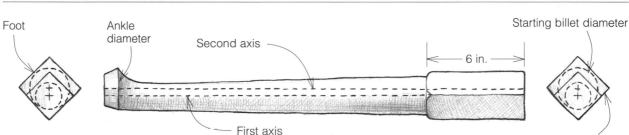

Foot

Ankle diameter

Second axis

First axis

6 in.

Starting billet diameter

Turn foot on second axis and shaft on first axis.

Shaded portion is removed from pommel before or after turning, depending on center locations.

Turning a Parallel-Axes Leg

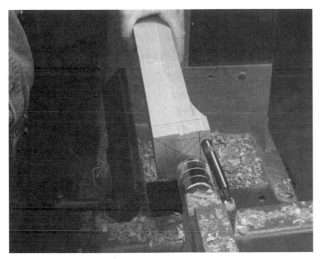

1. Mount the trimmed billet on the second axis and rotate it by hand to be sure it does not hit the tool rest.

2. Turn the foot. Make it slightly longer than necessary at this point (it will be corrected when the ankle is turned).

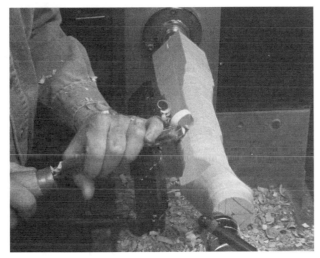

3. Remount on the first axis and turn the shaft and the ankle. Be careful when turning the top of the foot, which is an interrupted cove cut.

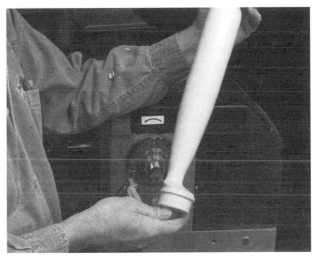

4. Sand, stain and finish the completed leg to taste.

Chair Parts

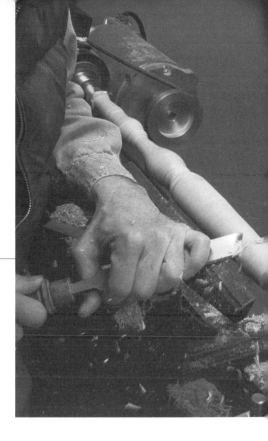

I've met a lot of woodworkers who have shied away from building chairs because some of the parts require turning. A common misconception is that the job is complicated and difficult. This is just not true. Turning chair parts is easy—anyone can do it. All it takes is the right technique, suitable wood and a little practice.

Many woodworkers consider maple and birch to be best-suited for chair parts because they are tight-grained and strong, although almost any hardwood will do. Regardless of the choice of wood, boards should be clear and with straight grain.

Typical parts for chairs include stretchers, arm posts, legs and back posts. The biggest challenge in making any of these parts is duplicating them with precision. Here again, a pattern stick or a master part is essential (see pp. 51-55). Remember, it's the location of the details that the eye catches. Variations in diameter and shape will go virtually unnoticed.

Stretchers and Arm Posts

A stretcher is the simplest chair part to turn. Stretchers run between legs or other stretchers to provide structural support to a chair. Tenons are turned on both ends and are often wedged for additional support. They're short enough that harmonic chatter isn't usually a problem. A stretcher is normally symmetrical, with the details on both ends being mirror images of each other.

Most turners find it difficult to turn duplicate details on both ends of a stretcher (or any spindle for that matter), but I have a nifty solution for dealing with this problem. I'm right-handed, so it's easier and more accurate for me to turn to the right (I also find that it's less intimidating to work near the tailstock). That being the case, I turn the right half of the stretcher first. With the right side finished, I reverse the stretcher in the lathe so that I can turn another right half (see photos below). If you are left-handed, simply work to the left.

Since many stretchers have a center groove, a small inaccuracy in duplication will never be noticed. The only critical measurement on a stretcher is the diameter of the tenons. To provide sufficient support, they must be sized to fit tightly in their mortises. I use an open-end wrench to size them perfectly (see pp. 54-55).

Turning a Stretcher

1. Chuck the stretcher between centers and turn round. Then find the midpoint of the stretcher and lay out the diameters.

2. Turn the right half of the stretcher first (or left half if you are left-handed). Here the author is sizing the tenon using a bedan and an open-end wrench.

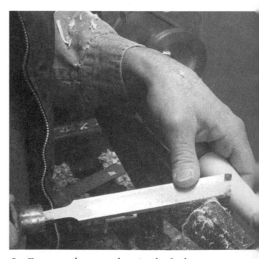

3. Reverse the stretcher in the lathe and turn the other half to match the first half.

Arm posts are used to support the arm and back of a chair—with the help of the spindles—in Windsor chairs and derivative styles. Arm posts often have more complicated details than the rest of the spindles and tend to mimic the turning style of the legs. But because they're short, arm posts are easy to turn. An arm post has a tenon on both ends, so you can use the same turning technique you would use for a stretcher.

Legs

Next to stretchers, chair legs are the simplest chair part to turn. A Windsor leg is probably the most common type of chair leg, and there are many variations on the style (see drawings below). Legs of this type may require you to employ a steady rest, depending on the type

WINDSOR CHAIR LEGS

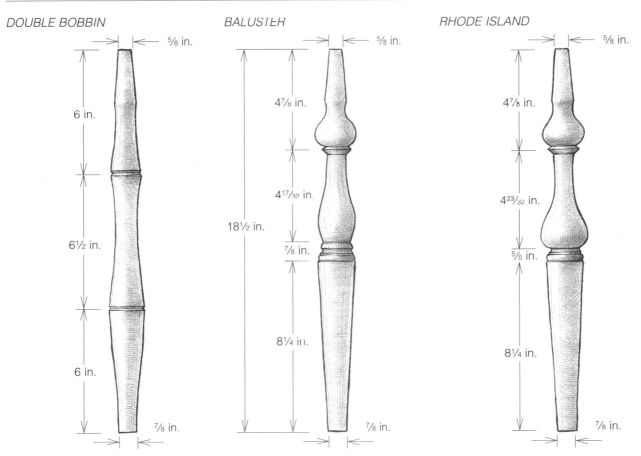

DOUBLE BOBBIN

5/8 in.
6 in.
6½ in.
6 in.
7/8 in.

BALUSTER

5/8 in.
4⅞ in.
4¹⁷/₃₂ in.
18½ in.
⅞ in.
8¼ in.
⅞ in.

RHODE ISLAND

5/8 in.
4⅞ in.
4²³/₃₂ in.
5/8 in.
8¼ in.
7/8 in.

of wood used and the length and diameter of the leg. It is easiest to test the first leg and reach for the steady rest if there is excessive chatter. Regardless of the wood, this is straight spindle turning all the way, with shear-cutting techniques carrying the day.

Using the photos on p. 72 as a guide, here's how to turn the leg. (To learn how to turn cabriole legs, see Chapter 5.) Start with a square billet of uniform size. Use a pattern stick or dividers and a ruler to lay out critical elements and diameters. Bring the billet just round for its entire length with a roughing-out gouge, then continue turning until you've reached a consistent major diameter (check it with calipers).

Work from the center toward the ends. Size the intermediate diameters first with a cutoff tool and calipers. Turn the intermediate diameters and save the smallest diameters for last. Working this way will allow the spindle to support itself better, with less harmonic chatter: You will only have to deal with the chatter at the very end, when finishing the smallest diameters, and that's where a steady rest may come in handy. Once all the diameters have been roughed in, clean up the details with a spindle gouge and skew chisel, then sand.

Turning a Windsor Chair Leg

1. Start with a square billet of uniform size and bring it just round with a roughing-out gouge. Continue turning until you've reached a consistent major diameter.

2. Work from the center toward the ends. Size the intermediate diameters first with a cutoff tool and calipers. Save the smallest diameters for last, so the spindle will support itself better, with less chatter.

3. Work the final details with the skew chisel, then sand.

74

Bent Back Posts

A bent back post is probably the most daunting of all chair parts to make, but it is actually quite easy to execute. The only real decision is whether to turn before or after bending. Most woodworkers bend the stock after turning. Bending after turning has two distinct advantages: First, the bend can be compound and extend into the back portion of the posts; second, no special chuck is necessary. The downside of this scheme is that there can be considerable grain-raising and splitting on the outside of the bend during steaming and bending.

Turning after bending is most common when a portion of the back remains square for joinery. The trick to turning a bent spindle is to keep the section to be turned straight in the lathe. To accomplish this, you'll need to make a special chuck to accept the curved portion of the leg and keep the other portion straight in the lathe. This chuck is basically a shallow plywood box with a notch in it to accept the bent portion of the back post. The other side of the box is hollow so that you can add sand or weights as a counterbalance to eliminate vibration. Sand is a better choice because it's easier to match the weight of the spindle. The whole setup resembles a broomstick when assembled. In use, the "broom" end is driven by the headstock, and the handle spins balanced on the tailstock. Obviously, speeds should be kept low (in the 1,000-rpm range).

This chuck allows the turning of bent spindles. It has a notch in it to accept the bent portion of the spindle, and it can be counterbalanced with sand or weights to eliminate vibration. In use, the "broom" end is driven by the headstock, and the handle spins balanced on the tailstock.

Bed Posts

Bed posts are among the biggest (and in the case of Sheraton posts, the longest) of all turnings encountered by the furniture maker. They are right on the small end of architectural turning because bed posts are a minimum of 2½-in. square and run upwards of 8 in. by 8 in. Today finding solid stock for such turnings can be quite a challenge. While gluing up stock is fine from a structural standpoint, I prefer to use one-piece billets.

As is always the case, whether a steady rest will be necessary depends much on the size and length of the turning. Many bed posts are robust in size and are left square for a good part of their length, so a steady rest can be dispensed with. In general, 1,200 rpm is the top speed for turning bed posts. Because of the weight of the billet, accurate centering is a must, and a good-sized spur center with sharp tines is advisable. While normal bed posts are within the capacity of most lathes, if you own a small lathe, you may have to make the post in two sections and join them together. This is simple to do and should not cause a problem when properly concealed. If the footboard, headboard and stretchers of the bed will be attached with mortise-and-tenon joints, it is best to mortise the pieces after turning. Mortises weaken the billet, increasing the chance of vibration and a possible split.

Turning a Short Bed Post

To turn a short bed post, start with a suitably sized billet (in this case about 2¾-in. square) and mark the centers carefully. The size and weight of the billet make it necessary to set the lathe to a low speed (800 to 1,000 rpm). A live center is very helpful in turning large work because it allows the work to spin freely while providing additional support. Apply plenty of tailstock pressure and check it frequently and tighten if necessary because the spur center tends to dig in deeper during the roughing-out stage. The photos below illustrate the process.

Turning a Long Bed Post

A bed with long posts, such as a Sheraton bed, is a challenging, fun project. The biggest challenge in executing this post is its size: The average post is between 75 in. and 80 in. tall, yet most lathes are limited to spindles of 39 in. or less. The simplest solution is to turn the post in two or more sections. I have a lathe of my own design that

Turning a Short Bed Post

1. Lay out the pommel with a pencil, a square and a ruler. You need only mark a square line on one side of the billet.

2. Use the toe of a skew to cut a shoulder at the bottom of the pommel.

3. Use a roughing-out gouge to bring the billet round.

uses a wood bed that can be made any length within reason, but I still prefer to turn a long post in two or more pieces. I do this not because it makes the turning easier or better; it is a matter of convenience for the owner of the bed. Turning the posts in two sections allows the bed to be dismantled for moving.

Other than making the post in two sections, making a long post is straight spindle turning; the only difference is the size and weight of the billet. Use straight stock, center the billet carefully, make sure the chucking is tight (check it often) and use low speeds (800 to 1,000 rpm). Because the actual turning process is about the same as turning a normal-length bed post (see photos on pp. 80 and 81), I'm going to focus here on making a concealed mortise-and-tenon joint (even a short bed post could need this joint if your lathe is small).

MAKING A CONCEALED MORTISE-AND-TENON JOINT

A properly placed and executed mortise-and-tenon joint does not take away from the structural integrity of the post, and only when it is apart will anyone know where the joint is. There are two things to keep in mind with a concealed mortise-and-tenon joint: the length and diameter of the tenon.

4. *Turn details in the post using a spindle gouge.*

5. *Sand and finish the completed post.*

The best location for the joint is at the transition point between elements on the turning. A typical Sheraton bed post has a square section, where the headboard or footboard is mortised in, and where the stretchers connect. It also has a turned top section and is usually capped with a finial, which provides an easy way to conceal chucking. While some posts are square all the way to the floor, most incorporate a turned leg and/or foot. For Sheraton posts turned in a very short lathe, it may be convenient to place a joint between the turned leg and the square section, another above the square section and another at the finial.

Because it will withstand the most stress, the joint between the square section and the leg should incorporate a healthy tenon diameter, and it should be liberally glued. The joint between the top and bottom is seldom structural, so I don't use any glue in there, and the same goes for the finial at the top. This way it can be taken apart so that the bed can be moved easily.

Turning a Long Bed Post

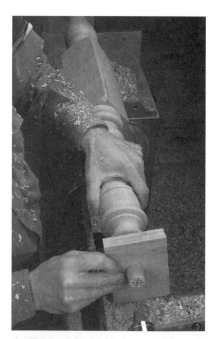

1. From 3¾-in. stock, use the toe of the skew to cut the transitions from square to round on the bottom section of the post.

2. Use the spindle gouge to shape the shoulders.

3. Turn a generous tenon, in this case 1-in. diameter by 4-in. long, at the top of the section. Check the size of the tenon with a test block drilled the same size as the mortise.

Turning the tenon

From 3¾-in. square stock (with sufficient extra length to allow for the tenon), turn the bottom portion of the post. Once the details have been turned and sanded, turn a generous tenon, in this case 1 in. diameter by 4 in. long at the top of the section. Use a test block with an appropriately sized hole drilled in it to check the size of the tenon. Then turn the top section of the post, paying close attention to the diameters on either side of the joint. Diameters must match between the two halves of the post, so careful turning with judicious use of calipers is necessary. You may also have to turn a tenon at the top of this section for the finial and drill a mortise to accept the 4-in. tenon on the bottom section of the post.

Drilling the mortise

Drilling the mortise straight (in line with the turning) and on center presents a challenge. There are two methods that I use. The first is to drill the mortise on the lathe, but this requires sufficient bed length to

4. Finish the details and sand.

5. Turn the top half of the post, carefully matching the diameter of the bottom element to the top element of the bottom post. Notice the tenon for the finial at the top of the post.

allow for the length of the bit, plus the post (see photo below). The size of the bit will depend on the diameter of the tenon, and the center-axis point marked on the post will help start the drill on center.

If drilling on the lathe is not an option, you can still mortise the bottom of the post perfectly off the lathe with a portable drill and the help of a shop-made jig (see drawing, facing page). The jig helps guide the bit straight into the post and makes the process easy. The jig is basically a cylinder with a hole drilled in each end. One hole is tapered to slip over the post. The other hole is drilled to match the tenon. To use the jig, just place it over the end of the post and drill. (Clamping the post to a bench greatly aids drilling.) An auger bit is best for this purpose because it is easy to guide into the jig. Once the

If your lathe is big enough to accept both the post and the drill bit, you can drill the mortise on the lathe.

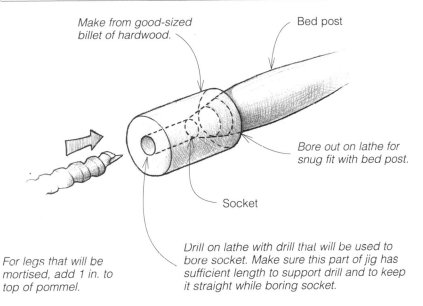

Make from good-sized billet of hardwood.

Bed post

Bore out on lathe for snug fit with bed post.

Socket

For legs that will be mortised, add 1 in. to top of pommel.

Drill on lathe with drill that will be used to bore socket. Make sure this part of jig has sufficient length to support drill and to keep it straight while boring socket.

mortise is drilled, check the fit. If things go awry, take heart: You have a second chance. Simply turn a plug, glue it in the hole and rebore the mortise. The whole process is shown in the photos on pp. 84 and 85.

If you encounter problems fitting the tenon, there are two things to check. First, the thick stock for a long bed post (usually at least 4-in. square to begin with) often tends to have high moisture content in the middle. Therefore, it is likely that the tenon will shrink after turning. On the turning I executed for the photo essay on pp. 84 and 85, the tenon was a press-fit with my test block. By the next day it was a loose fit. Second, bits tend to drill a bit oversize—especially in end grain. Therefore, a loose fit is common.

I have two solutions to a loose-fitting tenon. One is duct tape: A small piece carefully taped on the tenon will create a perfect fit. Another solution is to buy a couple of O-rings to match the diameter of the tenon (in this case, 1-in. diameter). O-rings can often be found in the plumbing department of most hardware stores or any plumbing supply house. Cut a small cove near the top and bottom of the tenon, snap the O-ring in place, and you'll get a perfect fit. Be sure to wax the mortise well so that the O-ring slides without tearing.

Drilling a Mortise Off the Lathe

1. *Turn the jig shown on p. 83. Scrape out the center to match the diameter of the bottom of the post.*

2. *Drill a hole in the center of the jig that matches the diameter of the tenon.*

3. *Check to make sure the bed post fits snug in the tapered socket.*

4. *Place the jig over the end of the post and drill. Clamping the post to a bench greatly aids drilling.*

5. *Once the mortise is drilled, check the fit. If things go awry, turn a plug, glue it in the hole and rebore the mortise.*

Decorative and Structural Columns

Many pieces of furniture incorporate columns, as both decorative elements and structural components. Decorative columns are common to clocks and cabinetry and other ornate pieces. Many types of furniture employ applied split columns (often called engaged columns) as decorative elements. The center column common to Philadelphia pie-crust tables, similar tea tables and plant stands is structural.

Engaged Columns

Depending on where an engaged column (typically decorative) is installed—whether on the face, an inside corner or an outside corner of the piece—the billet is split into half, quarter or three-quarter pieces, respectively. To split the turning, you could use a table saw or a bandsaw, but this can be dangerous. A safer, simpler solution is to use a paper glue joint when making the billet. To make a paper joint, insert brown kraft paper (shopping bags work well) between the pieces before they are glued together. (I've illustrated a few examples of how to glue up a billet for a split turning on p. 88.) A billet glued up in such a way allows you to turn identical elements in one shot, and the joint splits apart easily.

PAPER JOINTS FOR SPLIT TURNINGS

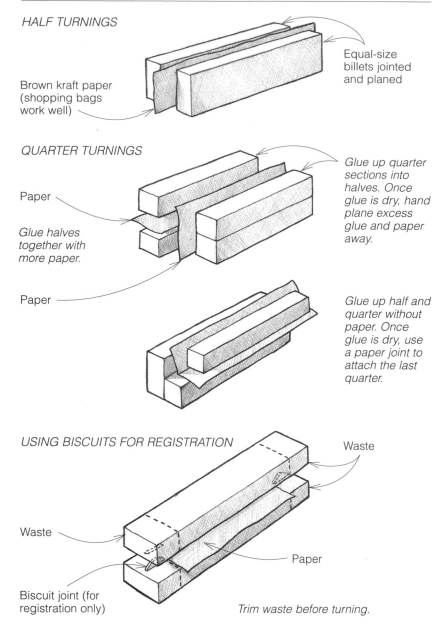

HALF TURNINGS

Brown kraft paper
(shopping bags
work well)

Equal-size
billets jointed
and planed

QUARTER TURNINGS

Paper

Glue halves
together with
more paper.

Paper

Glue up quarter
sections into
halves. Once
glue is dry, hand
plane excess
glue and paper
away.

Glue up half and
quarter without
paper. Once
glue is dry, use
a paper joint to
attach the last
quarter.

USING BISCUITS FOR REGISTRATION

Waste

Waste

Paper

Biscuit joint (for
registration only)

Trim waste before turning.

As in all glue joints, a joinery-level fit is necessary. So use a hand plane or a jointer on the edges of each piece to achieve a perfect match. Yellow or white glue will work fine for a paper joint, but they tend to soak through the paper in spots, making splitting the pieces apart difficult. That's why I prefer to use hide glue for paper joints. Not the liquid hide glue you buy at the hardware store in a bottle; I'm talking the real McCoy that's cooked in a glue pot. Hide glue doesn't soak through the paper as readily, and it's easier to split the pieces apart. Just insert a hot knife in the joint to reheat and liquefy the glue, and then separate the pieces.

Whatever glue you use, coat each joint and position the kraft paper between the joints. Then clamp up the billet, and leave it clamped tight until you are sure the glue is dry (hide glue will take a full 24 hours).

For quarter and three-quarter turnings, glue-up must be carefully thought out and done in stages. Stock must be carefully prepared so that the pieces remain aligned during glue-up and clamping. A tactic I have used successfully is to make the stock about 2 in. longer than necessary on each end and use biscuit joints in the very ends to register the pieces during glue-up and clamping (see bottom drawing, facing page). I do not insert paper between the joints where the biscuits are because this extra 2 in. will be cut off of the ends *before* turning. I have tried using only the biscuits to hold the billet together—without the paper joints—and trimming the excess after turning. The problem with this method is that the pieces tend to vibrate against each other in the middle section, causing excessive chatter. The paper joints allow the piece to turn like a solid billet.

For a perfect split turning, you'll want to chuck the billet in the lathe centered exactly on the parting line. This is one of the times that it is best to use a ring-shaped tailstock center (also called a cup point) and not a 60° point, for the latter might split the joint (for more on centers, see Appendix A). Once chucked, turning the piece is straightforward. To take apart the billet after turning, insert a sharp chisel into each joint and give it a hard rap with a mallet. The result will be two or more identical pieces from one billet.

Large, Hollow Columns

When making a large column (such as a column for a fireplace mantel), I've found that a coopered billet works well. A coopered billet is hollow in the center, which is useful both for the savings in materials and the lighter weight in the completed piece (see photo, p. 90). Coopered columns also hold up better outdoors than solid columns because there is less of a tendency for the wood to move with changes in humidity (coopered columns can be decorative or structural).

To make a coopered column that is tapered, you can taper the staves to give a taper to the starting billet that is close to the taper of the final column. But this is very time-consuming and requires a lot of jigs. Instead, I have found it easier to glue staves of sufficient thickness so that I can turn the billet and create the taper right on the lathe (this

Hose clamps are a handy, inexpensive clamping system for coopered columns. Laying the staves out on duct tape makes alignment for clamping easy. Shown here is a glued-up blank and the finished turning.

method works well for furniture-size columns). I cut the staves with a high-quality carbide blade in the table saw to produce accurate, smooth miters that need no further treatment.

The biscuit jointer is a great help in aligning all of the staves during glue-up. I use three biscuits: one in the center and one at each end. For small glue-ups, where biscuits are prohibitive, duct tape is a good alternative for aligning the staves during assembly. To use duct tape, lay out all of the staves on two strips of duct tape, apply glue and wrap up the assembly. The tape will hold things while you get the clamps arranged and tightened. I also use hose clamps (available at most hardware stores) to hold the staves tightly together during assembly (see photo left) or a Spanish windless, which is nothing more than a piece of stout rope with a stick to twist it until tight. Both methods give sufficient pressure to provide perfect glue lines.

Carved Columns

Furniture turnings often incorporate fluting, reeding and spiral motifs. Because these embellishments are most commonly associated with columns, it makes sense to discuss them here. This information may be readily applied to other spindle turnings, however.

Flutes are concave depressions in the surface of a column, running parallel to the center axis of the column. Reeding is a convex protrusion on the surface of a column, running parallel to the center axis of the column. Spiral carving takes many forms and often has multiple starts, oftentimes looking like strands of large-diameter rope twisted together.

These embellishments can be done by hand or machine (most commonly with a router), and the decision on which method to use lies with the craftsman. For those comfortable with hand tools, it will often be quicker to carve flutes, reeds or spirals in columns by hand rather than to set up a router and build the associated jigs. On the other hand, once the router is set up and the jigs built, any number of carvings may be made—and duplicated with staggering consistency.

FLUTING AND REEDING
Regardless of the method you use, indexing (see p. 8) is necessary for proper spacing of reeds and flutes. It is best to index all the way round the work, drawing pencil lines at whatever spacing the design calls for. This will ensure that the spacing is appropriate without having to make a lot of sample cuts.

The photos on the facing page show how to use hand methods to flute (but could just as well be applied to reeding). The only difference is that a V-chisel is used to start each reed, and each one is

Fluting by Hand

1. In conjunction with an indexing mechanism, use the tool rest to lay out the flute or reed pattern.

2. Following the pencil layout, use the tool rest to guide your chisel in cutting the flutes or reeds. Light blows with a carver's mallet work much better than trying to push the gouge by hand.

3. The fluted turning is ready for sanding and finishing.

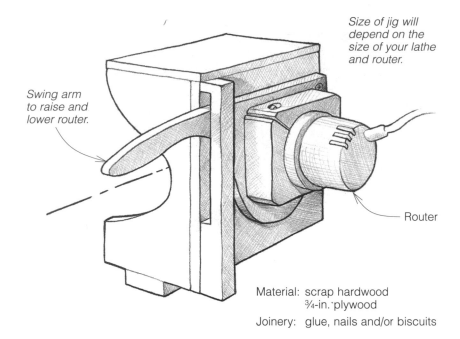

Swing arm
to raise and
lower router.

Size of jig will
depend on the
size of your lathe
and router.

Router

Material: scrap hardwood
¾-in. plywood
Joinery: glue, nails and/or biscuits

The swing arm of the jig is used to lower and raise the router onto the work. The jig is slid along the lathe bed to make the cuts.

brought to final shape with an in-cannel (bevel on the inside) gouge of the correct sweep. Flutes are done entirely with an out-cannel gouge (bevel on the outside) of the proper sweep.

To make uniform size flutes and reeds, I find it's easier to use a router jig mounted on the lathe (see drawing above). The jig shown in the drawing and photos is based on one made by my good friend Ed Young for some bed posts he turned several years ago. (For illustration purposes, the photo shows the jig mounted backwards. It would normally be turned 180° from this position. In the photo I am standing on the wrong side of the lathe so that you can see it.)

To cut the reeds, pilot bearings on either side of the bit ride on the work and control the depth of the cutter. The handle is used to lower the cutter slowly into the work (and raise it at the end of each reed), then the entire jig is slid along the work to mill each reed.

CARVING SPIRALS

While router jigs exist for cutting spirals, they vary greatly in quality, and the good ones tend to be expensive. I have always elected to do this job by hand because I have never had to make more than two at a time. (If you'll be doing a lot of spiral carving, you might want to invest in a jig.) The carving technique described here works well.

Carving Spirals by Hand

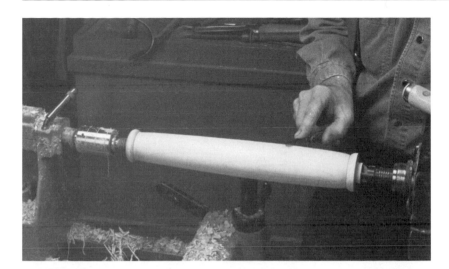

1. Lay out the spiral pattern, then place a knife edge on the turning at the helix angle of the spiral you want to achieve. Turn the lathe over by hand while pushing down on the knife.

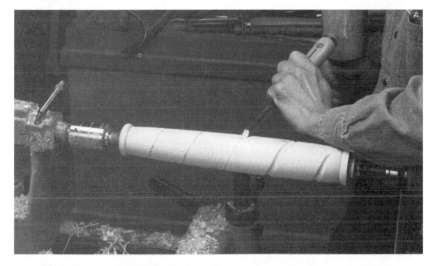

2. Use an in-cannel gouge and a mallet to carve out the spiral. If your design has wide, deep spirals, it might be a good idea to remove the initial material with a backsaw.

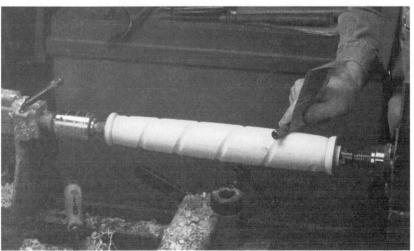

3. Sand the grooves with sandpaper wrapped around a rattail rasp (a dowel will also work well).

Start by laying out the desired spiral pattern. Then place a knife edge on the turning at the helix angle of the spiral you want to achieve. Turn the lathe over by hand while pushing down on the knife. The knife will scribe a helix up the turning. I usually make a second parallel helix right next to the first to make a road of sorts for my gouge. Use the indexing mechanism to line up the first and subsequent starts if the column is to have multiple spirals.

With the pattern laid out, use an in-cannel gouge and a mallet to carve out the spiral. If your design has wide, deep spirals, it might be a good idea to remove the initial material with a backsaw. Cut along the scribe lines to rough in the pattern. Then switch to the gouge.

Cutting Dovetail Slots in a Column

Columns for Philadelphia pie-crust tables, tea tables and similar structural columns often have three feet attached at the bottom of the column for mechanical strength. Attaching the feet is best done with a dovetail joint. The slots are made in the base of the column, and matching dovetails are cut in the legs so that they may be attached by sliding in from the bottom of the column.

Historically, the dovetails were cut with a backsaw and chiseled out in much the same way that a half-blind dovetail is cut by hand. Today, it is much quicker and more accurate with the router in the lathe.

All you'll need to build is a simple jig (see drawing at right). It is essentially a box that surrounds the work. The box has a wood key on the bottom that matches the gap in the lathe bed. A slot in the top of the jig matches a guide bushing on the router. I use a large carbide-tipped dovetail bit to mill the dovetail. The matching dovetail on the leg can be made in a router table with the same bit, or it can be cut on a table saw. I use the router table and hold the work with a tenoning jig (from my table saw) running in the miter slot.

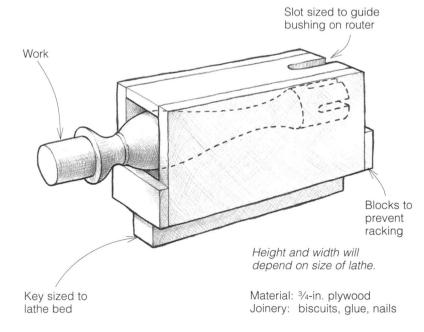

Work

Slot sized to guide bushing on router

Blocks to prevent racking

Height and width will depend on size of lathe.

Key sized to lathe bed

Material: ¾-in. plywood
Joinery: biscuits, glue, nails

Because one-half of the gouge is always cutting against the grain, some tearout is to be expected. Also, chiseling a perfect groove on a round surface is difficult. Therefore, you'll need to sand to even out the details and to clean up any spots where tearout occurred. To get into the groove, try wrapping the sandpaper around a dowel of suitable diameter (rattail rasps can also be used). Start with about 60-grit sandpaper and work your way up until you've achieved a satisfactory surface. The photos on p. 93 show the process.

Mount the router jig on the lathe bed and chuck a large dovetail bit in the router. Put the router in the jig and use the indexing mechanism to hold the column steady. For a lathe with 24 indexing positions, use every eighth hole; with 60 indexing positions, use every 20th hole. Then mill three dovetail slots in the base of the column.

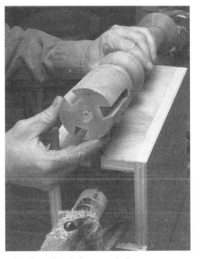

The finished dovetail slots are evenly spaced.

Pulls and Finials

One of my favorite ways to break up a piece of furniture and give it a custom look is to add hand-turned pulls and finials. I have always enjoyed adding this personal touch, and it allows me to use scraps of wood that I would otherwise burn—curly, blistered and bird's-eye woods, as well as burl.

Pulls can be either spindle or faceplate turned. Faceplate turning works best for larger pulls, which are held on the drawer front or door with a wood screw. I prefer spindle-turning for smaller pulls (and finials), where attachment with a screw does not work as well. For spindle-turned pulls, I like the traditional approach of turning a ¼-in., ⅜-in. or ½-in. tenon (depending on the size of the pull) on the back of the pull. A hole of matching size is drilled through the drawer front or door frame, and the pull is glued in place. For added security, you can saw a slot in the tenon and insert a wedge from the back as shown in the drawing on p. 98.

SPINDLE TURNED

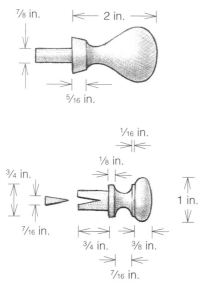

7/8 in.

2 in.

5/16 in.

1/16 in.

1/8 in.

3/4 in.

1 in.

7/16 in.

3/4 in.

3/8 in.

7/16 in.

For secure mounting, insert a wedge in the tenon.

FACEPLATE TURNED

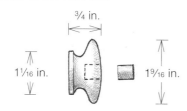

3/4 in.

1 1/16 in.

1 9/16 in.

Dowel of contrasting wood set into face of knob.

This knob can be made in any size and is excellent for large drawers that will hold a lot of weight.

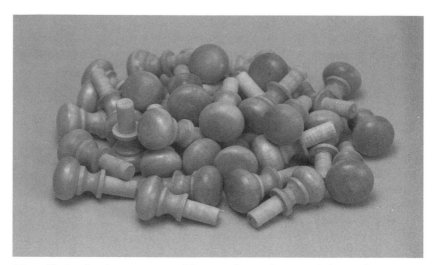

These Shaker knobs were turned from curly maple scraps left over from cutting out tabletop blanks.

Faceplate Turning Pulls and Finials

Generally speaking, the most beautiful wood for faceplate-turned pulls will be found in tangentially sawn lumber. The exceptions are curly and blistered woods and species that tend to have a beautiful ray structure, such as oak and sycamore. For these woods, I've learned that quartersawn stock creates the best-looking knobs. As I'm working with wood for any project, I throw any promising scrap in a box for pulls.

To prepare a series of pulls for turning, use dividers to lay out the circles on blanks. Bandsaw the blanks larger than the layout circles (they will be trimmed down to size in the lathe) and drill holes in their center at the drill press (it's easy to pick up the center from the mark left by the dividers). Thread a blank onto the screw chuck and bring it just round (see left photo, facing page). A ¼-in. bowl gouge is very handy for faceplate turning pulls. You can get by with a spindle gouge, but there's more likelihood of a catch when cutting against the grain. After turning round, turn the pull to shape. I trim the screw chuck away to match the base diameter of the pull so that on subsequent pulls, I won't have to use calipers to size the base—the screw chuck will serve as a template (see right photo, facing page). After shaping, sand and finish the pull. The same methods and chucking for pulls can be used for finials.

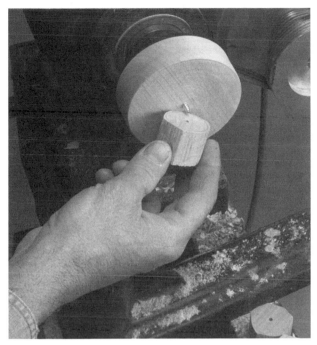

Thread a blank onto the homemade screw chuck, then turn it round using a ¼-in. bowl gouge.

To make duplication easier, trim the screw chuck to match the base diameter of the knob. You won't have to use calipers to size the base—the screw chuck will be the guide.

To faceplate turn pulls, I use a homemade screw chuck. The foundation of this screw chuck is a glue block. And because glue blocks are the basis of a lot of different chucking systems, I always keep a stack of bandsawn blocks ready at the lathe.

Making a screw chuck is easy. Start by mounting a disk of wood to a small faceplate (3 in. diameter or smaller). I cut my disks from 6/4 stock and mount them to the faceplate with 1 in. screws. This way there's plenty of wood above the screw. Mount the faceplate in the lathe and scrape the face of the glue block square. I use a try square or a straightedge to make sure the face is dead flat and square to the headstock spindle. Next, drill a small hole for the screw in the center of the glue block with a bit secured in a drill chuck mounted in the tailstock. With some care in starting, this will give you a hole at the exact center of the block. Now remove the faceplate from the lathe and thread a sheet-metal screw (don't use a drywall screw because they're too brittle and prone to breakage) through the hole in the back of the face plate. Epoxy or super glue will prevent the screw from coming out while you're mounting the work (the photos on p. 100 show the process).

Making a Homemade Screw Chuck

1. Screw a disk of wood to a small faceplate (3 in. in diameter or smaller).

2. Mount the faceplate in the lathe and scrape the face of the glue block square.

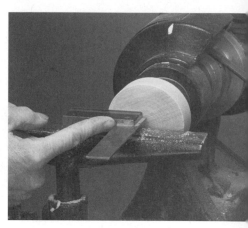

3. Use a try square to make sure the face is flat and square to the headstock spindle.

4. Drill a hole for the screw in the center of the glue block with a bit in a drill chuck mounted in the tailstock. Use care in starting so that you end up with a hole at the exact center of the block.

5. Remove the faceplate from the lathe and thread a sheet-metal screw through the hole in the center.

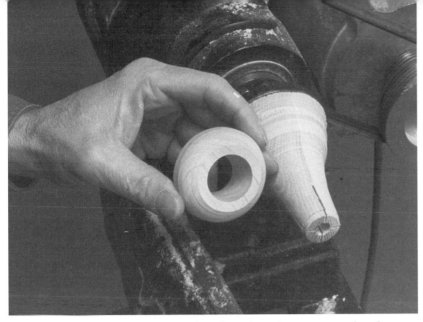

This chuck is a simple shop-built collet. The hole in the center matches the diameter of the tenon on the pull to be turned. The ring is forced down over the tapered end and closes the "jaws" around the tenon.

Spindle Turning Pulls and Finials

Given a choice, I'll spindle turn pulls and finials because I like to turn a tenon on the end for mounting. When turning multiple pulls, I start with a billet that's twice the length of one pull, plus a bit extra for parting off. I then chuck the billet between centers to turn a tenon on each end. This tenon can then be gripped in a chuck for turning the pull itself.

Chucking presents more of a challenge with spindle-turned pulls. One solution is to use a commercial chuck (such as the One Way or Nova chuck) to grip the tenon so you can turn the knob. If you're on a budget, you can make your own chuck. With a homemade wooden chuck there is never a danger of damaging your turning tools if you accidentally hit the chuck (like you would if you hit the spinning metal jaws of a commercial chuck). And you don't have to worry about receiving a nasty whack from a spinning jaw. What is more, just like the screw chuck, the chuck body can be turned down to the base diameter of the first pull, so you can match subsequent pulls to the base, negating the need for calipers.

The chuck I make is a simple shop-built collet (see photo above), much like the collet that holds bits in your router. To make one like it, mount a suitable-sized billet on a faceplate with sheet-metal screws. Drill a hole in the center to match the diameter of the tenon on the pull (or finial) you are going to hold. Turn a gentle taper on the outside of the chuck. To create the "jaws" of the chuck, make two perpendicular cuts across the center of the end with a backsaw. Cut a little farther back than the length of the tenon the chuck will hold.

After making the jaws, turn a compression ring of suitable diameter from wood. This ring is then forced down over the tapered end to compress the jaws tightly against the tenon and hold the blank securely in place. Although a metal ring of suitable size often can be found, I find that it's easier to turn one from wood. The ring is best faceplate turned, but remember to keep the cross section robust for strength. You may be tempted to use a hose clamp in place of the ring, but I've found that a hose clamp does not give anywhere near the compression strength of a ring on a taper.

Making a pull or finial is simple. First, chuck the billet between centers and turn a tenon on each end. Then mount the tenon on one end of the billet in the chuck. Place the compression ring over the chuck and tap it with a mallet to compress the jaws. Use a cutoff tool to part the billet in the center and turn the first pull. When you're finished with the first pull, remove it and mount the second. You may have to rap the ring a few times with a mallet to loosen it. The photos on the facing page highlight the process. Follow the same procedures for the second and subsequent pulls. The same materials and procedures will work to turn finials (see photo below).

This finial was turned using a homemade collet chuck, with the aid of a pattern stick.

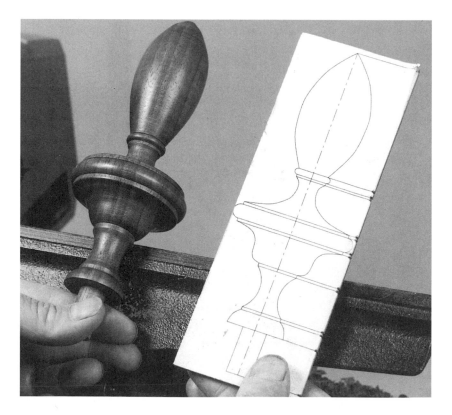

Turning Pulls

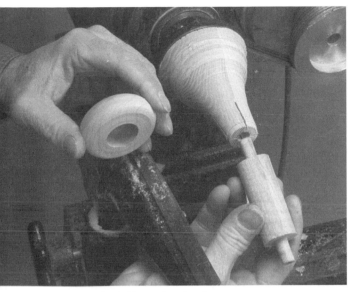

1. *Mount the billet in the chuck.*

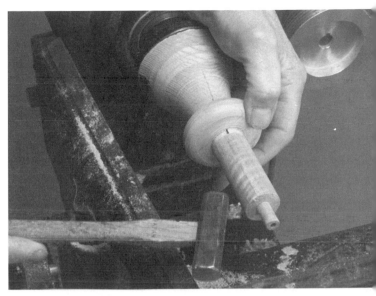

2. *Tap the ring with a mallet to tighten the jaws.*

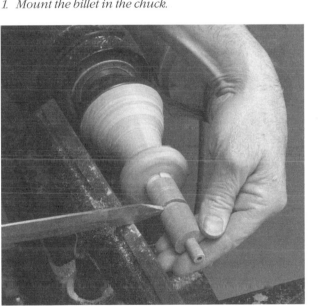

3. *Use a cutoff tool to part the billet in the center and then turn the first pull. Be sure and turn the chuck down to match the base diameter of the pull so that you match subsequent pulls without using calipers.*

4. *When you're finished with the first pull, remove it and mount the second. To loosen the ring, you may need to give it a few sharp raps with a mallet.*

Applied
Moldings

One of the simplest yet most elegant ways to incorporate distinctive details into the furniture you build is with applied moldings. Applied moldings are quick and easy to turn and can be as simple as a corner block (an architectural embellishment put at the upper corners of the trim around a door frame) or as elaborate as a medallion (an oval or circular molding used to frame an ornamental fixture such as a chandelier). These and other types of decorative elements can be interesting, profitable work for the wood turner and can be accomplished with a faceplate alone or with the addition of a simple shop-made chuck. Whether you use a chuck or not will depend on what item you're turning and how many you plan to make.

Single Pieces

If you're planning on making just a few small items like an escutcheon (an ornamental or protective plate, usually seen around a keyhole) or a rosette (a painted, carved or sculpted ornament that suggests the petals of a rose), it's often easiest simply to fasten a blank directly to the faceplate with double-sided tape or a paper joint (see pp. 88 and 89 for more on paper joints). Although many turners use double-sided tape in lieu of the paper joint, I still lean toward paper and glue. Call me old-fashioned, but I prefer the extra holding power glue offers, plus I like the fact that I have a bit of open time to slide things around into perfect position—with double-sided tape, you get one shot. And when it comes time to unchuck, the paper joint also comes apart easier.

If you do decide to use double-sided tape, there are a couple of things to keep in mind. First, make sure to use cloth-based tape. Most of the "carpet tape" sold at local hardware stores is foam-based, which doesn't offer sufficient holding power. Cloth- or fabric-based tape is available through industrial distribution chains or from mail-order catalogs. (There are even some tapes designed specifically for turning, such as Permacell brand, available from Craft Supplies—800-551-8876). Second, you must make sure that adequate clamping pressure has been applied to the tape for proper adhesion. You can do this with clamps, a bench vise or even the tailstock. And finally, because you're taping the piece directly to the faceplate, it needs to be perfectly flat. If your faceplate has a raised lip at the edge (like mine), you can overcome this problem by screwing a thin block of wood to it and then scraping it flat.

Multiple Pieces

For projects that require multiple pieces that are identical in shape (such as corner blocks for trimming out a room, or drawer fronts for a spice cabinet), I often use a screw chuck (see p. 100) or a nest chuck. As the name implies, a nest chuck has a pocket in which the blank "nests" for turning. The chuck is just a scrap of wood fastened to the faceplate with a set of cleats to hold the blank. Three of the cleats are glued and nailed to the plywood to form a U. To make it easy to take blanks in and out of the chuck, the final cleat is ripped in half at an angle. After nailing one half to the chuck, the other serves as a wedge to capture the blank in the chuck. The photos on the facing page illustrate the process.

One other thing. To use a nest chuck, it's vital that all the blanks be uniform in size. Because of this, I like to cut all the blanks at one time. And I always cut a few extra in case of mistakes.

Turning a Corner Block with a Nest Chuck

1. Fasten a piece of plywood to the faceplate, then glue and nail three cleats to the plywood to form a U.

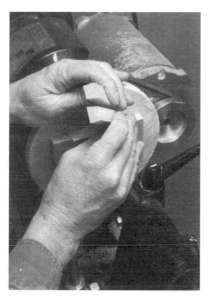

2. Rip the last cleat in half at an angle to make it easy to take blanks in and out of the chuck.

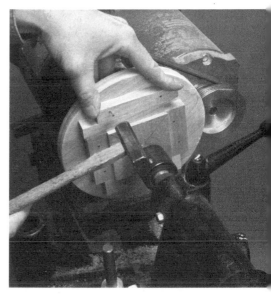

3. Nail one half of the cleat to the chuck.

4. The other half of the cleat serves as a wedge to capture the blank in the chuck.

5. As long as all the blanks are the same size, the nest chuck will hold them tightly.

Curved Moldings

Another simple way to make identical parts (such as sections of curved molding) is to start with a "frame" glued up of wide, mitered sections. The important thing here is to make sure the frame pieces are wide enough for the molding. The best way I've found to handle this is to start with a full-scale drawing of the molding, then sketch out the mitered sections.

Making a Curved Molding

1. To make identical sections of curved molding, start with a chuck, which in this case is simply a circle of plywood of the appropriate diameter mounted on a faceplate. Paper joint mitered pieces to the chuck. Make sure the pieces are wide enough for the molding.

2. Once the glue dries, bandsaw the work to a rough circle to match the chuck and mount it on the lathe.

Start by mitering the pieces and paper jointing (double-sided tape is okay, too) them to a circle of plywood of appropriate diameter mounted on a faceplate. Once the glue is dry, bandsaw the work even with the plywood circle (chuck). Once the molding is turned, all it takes is a chisel inserted between the molding and the chuck and a sharp rap of a mallet to remove a finished section. The process is shown in the photos on the facing page and below.

3. *Turn the molding. This can be done inboard or outboard, depending on the size of the molding and your lathe.*

4. *Insert a chisel between the molding and the faceplate and a give it a sharp rap with a mallet to remove a finished section.*

Tabletops

A circular tabletop opens up a whole range of design possibilities for a furniture maker and possibly a whole new area of work for a turner. All sorts of tabletops—tops for folding tea tables, candlestands, plant stands and a host of others—can be turned entirely on the lathe.

There are three factors that make turning a tabletop different from a typical faceplate turning. First of all, most tabletops are large (at least 14 in. in diameter) and so will need to be turned outboard with a floor-stand rest. Second, because of the size of such a turning, you'll need a large spindle and a low lathe speed. And third, making the blank for the top requires great care during glue up.

Outboard Turning

The main thing that separates tops from other types of turnings is size—because they're large, most tabletops have to be turned outboard. You'll need a suitable tool support. Some lathes have a swing-head design, which allows the headstock to be turned at a right angle to the bed (see p. 11). A swing head allows larger-diameter faceplate work to be swung in front of the bed, and the normal tool base can be used with an extension casting. The problem is that the diameter necessary for most tabletops is beyond the tool base/rest capacity of a swing-head lathe. Some lathe models have an outboard rest that attaches to the machine itself, which allows large outboard turnings—diameters of 22 in. to 40 in.

If your lathe has neither of these features, or if you're turning an extra-large top, you'll need to turn outboard with a floor-stand rest. A floor-stand rest does not have the rigidity of a normal tool rest, especially on large-diameter work, and the leverage required for a gouge or shear cut can tip the rest into the work. The consequences of such a mishap could be disastrous. Even though most tabletops require only light scraping cuts anyway, if you use a floor-stand tool rest, you'll need an even lighter touch. If things go awry while scraping lightly, you can usually let up on the pressure when you feel the rest tip—before things get out of hand.

Circular tabletops, like the one on this Shaker candlestand, can be turned outboard on the lathe. Photo by Robert Marsala.

Spindle Size and Speed

Another consideration for accomplishing a turning the size of a tabletop is the size of the spindle. In general, the bigger the turning, the bigger the spindle required. A large, heavy turning, for instance, should not be done on spindles smaller than 1 in., with 1⅛ in. to 1½ in. being much better.

When turning a tabletop, not only will you have to consider the spindle size of your lathe, but you'll also need to maintain a low speed for the turning. A large outboard turning demands speeds in the range of 50 to 350 rpm. Unfortunately, although many lathes can accommodate a large outboard turning, some do not have sufficiently low speeds to allow outboard work of any size to be done safely (many have a low speed of 600 rpm). Even though the trend in the last five years has been to put low-speed capacity on most lathes, with many older lathes (and some new ones), you'll have to reduce the speed by replacing the standard AC motor with a DC or by installing a counter shaft (see pp. 10 and 11 for more on controlling lathe speed).

Meticulous Glue Up

Careful preparation of the blank for a top is a must. To get a sufficiently wide blank for a tabletop, you'll more than likely have to glue up stock. If you do, take great pains in making the joint. Failure of a glue joint could be disastrous, so it's important to ensure perfectly jointed surfaces on the stock. I use a yellow or white glue, such as Titebond or Elmers, because of its strength. After glue up, carefully bandsaw the blank to a circle. This way the blank will have better initial balance when you begin turning.

Because only one face of the blank will be turned, it is only necessary to joint and/or plane one side of the blank after glue up. You simply have to clean up the side the faceplate will attach to. To help strengthen the glue joint, I like to glue a large square block to the bottom of the blank before attaching the faceplate. This allows me to use long screws, which will go through the block and a bit into the

Turning a Top for a Tea Table

1. *Cut a glue block of sufficient size, attach it to a faceplate and scrape the block flat. Then glue and screw the assembly to the blank.*

2. *Make the initial cuts with a scraper to flatten the top.*

4. *Use a straightedge to check the surface for flat.*

5. *With the lathe running, sand the top.*

tabletop blank. I also try to use only two boards in a tabletop blank, with the glue joint near the center. I do this so that the backing block will overlap both halves, further strengthening the glue joint.

Attach a suitable-size block (it can be bandsawn round or left square) to a faceplate and scrape it flat. Then drill each corner of the block to accept the screws that will attach the block (with faceplate)

3. Use a bowl gouge to remove a good amount of waste. If you're using a floor-stand tool rest, however, it's a good idea to avoid the gouge and only use light scraping; otherwise, heavy pressure could tip the rest into the spinning work.

6. After turning and sanding, finish the top.

to the blank. Then glue and screw the assembly to the blank. For added strength, change the screw in the faceplate, one at a time, to a longer screw that goes slightly into the blank. Allow the glue to dry, and you're ready to begin turning. The photos above show the process.

Part Three

APPENDICES

Appendix A
Holding Material on the Lathe

Most wood turners are always looking for the ultimate chuck—the one that will do everything. But no one chuck will hold everything, and many chucks are necessary if a wide variety of work is to be held. As you've probably noticed, I prefer homemade chucks. Beyond a factor of cost (their price is infinitesimal), they almost always work better than their commercial-made cousins. I have endeavored throughout this book to show homemade and improvised chucks, but in this section I will focus on commercial-made chucks.

Centers

The oldest and simplest way to hold work in the lathe is between two centers: one is mounted in the headstock spindle, and the other is mounted in the tailstock. Centers are fast, reliable and allow unlimited chucking and unchucking, which is an advantage for trial-fitting parts and applying finishes.

DRIVE CENTERS

The drive, or spur, center mounts in the lathe headstock and both holds and rotates the work. On most lathes, the shaft of the center is a Morse taper that fits in a matching socket in the spindle (for more on Morse tapers, see below). The business end of the drive center is a point, which is surrounded by spurs (often called tines). The point should protrude 1/16 in. to 1/8 in. above the face of the tines to ensure that the work is centered before the tines bite in. On better drive centers, the center point is adjustable so that the amount it protrudes above the tines can be changed with the needs of the turning situation, and it may be replaced when necessary. The center point should protrude a bit more for larger turnings and softer wood than it would for small turnings and harder wood.

Morse Tapers

A lathe with a Morse taper in its spindle is more useful than one without. Unlike threaded spindles, Morse tapers are universal, so you won't be limited to accessories made by your lathe manufacturer. On a quality lathe, both the drive and tailstock centers mount in the lathe by means of a Morse taper.

An American innovation, the Morse taper is used commonly in machinery produced worldwide because it is a sure, trouble-free method of mounting accessories in machine spindles. Technically, the taper is on the center, drill chuck or other accessory you want to mount in the lathe. A matching socket is machined in the spindle.

A Morse taper and its matching socket are about 3° inclusive, which is just sufficient taper to provide a locking action once driven into the socket. But it's not so strong that it won't release when an equal, opposite force is applied. Morse tapers come in sizes from #0 through #7, and the actual degree of taper is slightly different for each size. Wood lathes commonly have tapers ranging from #0 to #3, with #2 being the most common.

Accessories with Morse tapers expand the capabilities of your lathe. Shown here (from left) are a crotch center, a drill bit, a cup center and two drive centers.

You can adapt small Morse tapers to larger spindles using Morse-taper sleeves.

Drive centers are sold in both two- and four-spur models. Though four-spur drive centers are more common, I prefer the two-spur variety. It drives as well as a four-spur and can be oriented for equal and positive drive no matter what the contour of the end of the turning billet. A four-spur center will drive on only one tine when work is not square, which can often cause the work to go off center and even kick out of the lathe in extreme cases (see photo at right). Fortunately, it is a simple matter to modify a four-spur center by grinding two of the tines away.

Each tine of a spur center comes to a chisel point. It is vital that the chisel edges not be in line with each other, or the center will work more like a wedge, splitting the work. If the tines become dull or damaged, they can be ground back to a chisel edge (grind on the bevel edge only).

It is not usually necessary to pound the center into the work, nor is it necessary to saw lines into the end of the billet to achieve positive drive. Pressure from the tailstock will ensure that the tines bite in sufficiently. Even on small lathes, there is tremendous mechanical advantage in the screw-thread mechanism of the tailstock hand wheel. If you're using a 60° point on a live or dead center in the tailstock, it may be advantageous to tap the billet lightly with a wooden mallet when first mounting it. This will ensure that the tines bite in without the tailstock center having to dig in too deeply.

If you do small work, such as doll-house furniture parts, you may want to invest in a mini drive center because a standard drive center is large and will get in the way. A mini drive center has an outside diameter in the ⅜-in. to ½-in. range.

Drive centers with two or four spurs mount in the headstock spindle. A two-spur center (left) holds an unsquared end of a billet more securely than the four spur model (right).

TAILSTOCK CENTERS

A tailstock center mounts in the tailstock spindle to center and support the work. The end that sticks into the billet is either a 60° point or a cup center, which is a small center point surrounded by a raised ring. The outside ring of the cup center holds grease and prevents the work from splitting. But it has been my experience that a 60° point has no greater tendency to split work than a cup point. What's more, a 60° point holds in a much smaller area, which often is an advantage, and its simple construction allows it to hold up better in day-to-day use. About the only time a cup point is really needed is for special situations, such as a split segmented turning (see Chapter 8), where the fragile paper joint makes splitting the turning a real possibility.

There are two types of tailstock centers: dead centers and live centers. A dead center is relatively inexpensive, and many lathes include a dead center in the standard accessory kit. The center is stationary, so it must be lubricated to reduce friction and burning. A dab of grease will do. But no matter how much and how often you apply the grease, some burning with a dead center is to be expected.

A dead center consists of a simple pivot on which the work spins. Many lathes include such a center in the standard accessory kit. Dead centers must be lubricated to reduce friction and burning.

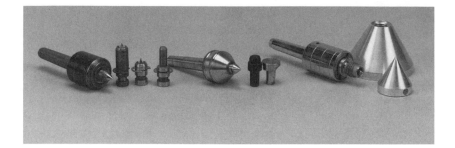

The center point of a live center spins on a bearing, so there is no need for lubrication, and burning is eliminated. Shown here is a sampling of live centers.

A better alternative to a dead center is a live center. On a live center, a bearing (usually a double-row bearing) allows the center point to spin with the billet (see photo above). Because of this, there is no need for lubrication, and burning is eliminated. Also, since friction isn't a problem with a live center, much greater force can be exerted on the work, so it will be held more securely.

Better live centers (and more expensive) are sold with two or three interchangeable points. The cup center and 60° point are the two traditional point options. (Metalworking supply houses offer 60° live centers at bargain prices.) Some live centers also have a third insert, which is flat-faced. This is used for special tasks, such as holding a bowl in a jam chuck or metal spinning, and is of little value to the furniture maker.

Faceplates

For work that cannot be supported (or that you don't want to support) by a tailstock, a faceplate is usually the answer. A faceplate is basically a disk that is threaded onto the lathe headstock spindle. Many faceplates are made from cast aluminum today, which is fine for most situations. But aluminum should not be used for large-diameter, heavy work (diameters above 18 in.). For these situations, there is no replacement for the density and strength of cast-iron or steel faceplates (see photo at left).

Faceplates are used to mount flat work on the headstock spindle.

Holes around the periphery of the faceplate allow work to be fastened to the plate with screws. Better faceplates are not flat but rather have a ridge around the outer edge, which allows the plate to seat flat on uneven surfaces much better. Common diameters for faceplates are 3 in., 6 in. and 9 in. For some reason, many woodworkers think they need a large faceplate—6 in. or larger. But the fact is that the small, 3-in. faceplate (often called a bowl chuck) will serve you much better. Bowl chucks are so handy that I recommend buying four to six of them so that you do not have to mount and unmount them all the time.

Faceplates are made to fit standard spindles, but you can make faceplates for oddball lathes if you can find a nut that fits the spindle. Simply have a welding shop weld a large, heavy, flat washer to the nut and drill and countersink evenly spaced holes around the periphery of the washer for screws.

To prevent work from flying off faceplates while turning, it's imperative to make sure the work is screwed securely in place. Traditionally, the common wood screw was used for this purpose, but sheet-metal screws work much better. Sheet-metal screws have straight bodies with a 45° thread profile that bites into wood aggressively. What is more, they are mildly heat treated, which gives them added toughness. As a minimum, a #10 sheet-metal screw should be used, with #12 or even #14 being better. I use #12 screws: 1 in. for the lion's share of my work, and 1½ in. when extra security is needed. Under no circumstances should you use drywall screws. They are hard and brittle and could snap under a heavy load.

Since most bowl chucks only have three holes around the circumference, it's a good idea to drill and countersink an extra hole between each of the originals for a total of six. This allows six screws in demanding situations, greatly increasing the holding power.

Scroll Chucks

Two scroll chucks designed especially for wood turning are the Nova chuck, which was the first on the market, and the Oneway, which is a close copy of the Nova (see top photo at right). Oneway, however, goes to the extra expense of case-hardening both the scroll and bottom jaws, as well as nickel-plating the chuck body. The hardening should give longer wear, and the plating provides self-lubrication and rust resistance. Nova, however, has the greatest variety of jaws, is the least expensive and has a very complete instruction manual. Because Nova was the original wood-turning scroll chuck, I will explain its operations and point out any differences of the Oneway.

Although the Nova scroll chuck has its roots in metalworking, it differs significantly from its ancestors. It is much lighter in design and has safety jaws that cannot fly out of the chuck body at the high speeds encountered in wood turning. A 4-in. diameter steel body encases four jaws (rather than the three in its metalworking cousin) that open or close in unison by the action of a circular scroll plate (see bottom photo at right). The Nova chuck uses steel levers that fit into holes to turn the scroll plate: one lever fits in the scroll itself, and the second set in the chuck body. For this reason such chucks are often called "lever chucks."

The Nova (left) and Oneway (right) scroll chucks are nearly identical, right down to their diameters and jaw sizes. These commercial chucks are made specifically for wood turning.

The scroll of each chuck engages the rack on the bottom of the base jaw, moving it in or out, depending on what direction the scroll is turned. (The scroll for the Nova is on the right; the Oneway is on the left.)

JAWS

For wood turning, a four-jaw scroll chuck is much more satisfactory than the three-jaw variety usually used in metalworking. Four jaws grip squares nicely but still hold round stock well. (It is tempting to use a surplus metalworking chuck, but don't do it. Even if the metalworking chuck has four jaws, they are not designed for holding wood. Besides being real knuckle-busters, the jaws are too small and tend to indent wood severely without ever centering it.)

A good-quality scroll chuck will have a two-piece jaw design: a base and a top. (Nova borrowed its two-piece jaw design from metalworking chucks.) The base jaws always stay in the chuck body, and the top jaws are bolted to the base jaws with socket-head screws. The two-piece design means the top jaw can easily be changed to accommodate any turning situation and allows the top jaw to hold over a much greater surface area.

There is a wide variety of top jaws available, from small to large to specialty jaws. One set of jaws for a medium-grip range is supplied with both the Nova and Oneway chucks, and two or more additional sizes are available at extra charge (see chart below). On both the Nova and Oneway chucks, an aluminum plate with holes tapped into it can be mounted in place of the jaws. The aluminum plate is cut into four sectors. By screwing rubber posts (what I call rubber baby buggy bumpers) to the plate at strategic positions, both round

Scroll Chucks				
Chuck	**Small Jaws**	**Medium Jaws**	**Large Jaws**	**Accessories**
Nova	$^{15}/_{16}$ in. to $2^1/_{16}$ in. Exp. $^3/_8$ in. to $1^1/_2$ in. Comp.	2 in. to 3 in. Exp. $^3/_4$ in. to $1^1/_2$ in. Comp.	$3^7/_8$ in. to $4^1/_2$ in. Exp. $3^3/_8$ in. to $3^5/_8$ in. Comp.	11- and 16-in. rubber bumper jaws Step jaws Spigot jaws Polypropylene jaws Pin jaws Screw center Spur center
Oneway	$^7/_8$ in. to $2^1/_4$ in. Exp. $^5/_{16}$ in. to $1^{13}/_{16}$ in. Comp.	2 in. to 3 in. Exp. 2 in. to 3 in. Comp.	$3^3/_4$ in. to $5^3/_8$ in. Exp. $3^1/_4$ in. to $4^1/_4$ in. Comp.	12-in. rubber bumper jaws Screw center Spur center
Exp. = Expansion hold Comp. – Compression hold				

and odd shapes can be held in the lathe (see top photo at right). Oneway's rubber posts have a hardened-steel core and a dovetail shape, which tends to pull work down onto the face of the aluminum plate. Nova's straight-sided rubber posts do not pull work onto the chuck face as well.

Rubber baby buggy bumper jaws are not intended for heavy primary turning, especially at large distances from the chuck face. They are really designed for bowl turners: You can hold a turned bowl by the rim so that light cutting and sanding can be done on the base to remove the chucking marks left during primary turning. They can be used for primary turning of thin, odd-shaped objects, if you restrict yourself to light cuts. Because they can grip square or rectangular pieces, they are also perfect for turning corner blocks.

Nova also offers polypropylene plastic Pro-Jaws, which are very useful for production situations. They are essentially polypropylene plastic blocks that bolt to the bottom jaws with socket-head screws. The plastic can then be worked with a scraper to the exact shape of the work to be held. The result is a perfectly fitting chuck from a soft, nonmarring plastic that will leave nary a trace that the work was ever gripped. Plastic jaws are a bit pricey at about $25 per set, but for a production job they can pay for themselves in a hurry. These jaws will also fit the Oneway chuck, but you'll need to be careful because you won't be able to use Oneway's safety locks, which hold the jaws on the chuck (for more on safety, see p. 124).

While you may think of scroll chucks as gripping by compressing around the outside of the work (compression hold), they work just as well by expanding inside a recess in the work (expansion hold). Wood-turning scroll-chuck jaws are angled on the outside. By scraping a dovetailed (undercut) recess in the work, the chuck can be expanded to securely hold under the recess.

One problem about lever chucks is knowing which way to turn the two levers for tightening. This can be most irksome when all you want to do is tighten the chuck to snug up the piece a bit. All it takes is one wrong turn, and your workpiece is falling on the floor. As a reminder, I engraved an arrow on the scroll. Turning the lever in the direction of the arrows moves the jaws inward for a compression hold; turning in the opposite direction will tighten for an expansion hold (see bottom photo at right).

Both the Nova and the Oneway come with a screw-chuck accessory. I use mine often for stool seats and escutcheons, among others. Both companies also offer a spur center that can be gripped in the chuck in the same manner as the screw-chuck accessory. The spur center allows you to accomplish spindle turning without dismounting the chuck. But I find the chuck body gets in the way much of the time, so I dismount the chuck and use a standard spur center for anything

Both Nova (right) and Oneway (left) offer for their scroll chucks what the author calls rubber baby buggy bumper jaws. Rubber posts are screwed to the four sections of an aluminum plate—in any configuration—to hold an odd shaped object.

Engraving an arrow on the scroll chuck will help you remember which way to turn the lever to tighten or loosen.

To prevent the jaws from opening beyond the grip of the scroll, the Nova chuck (left) has a set screw in the number-one jaw keyway. The Oneway (right) has a pin on the underside of one of the four top jaws that engages a slot in the jaw keyway.

but a very quick spindle job. This feature might be interesting, however, to someone who owns a lathe without a Morse taper in the headstock and has no source of spur centers.

SAFETY FEATURES

Scroll chucks from both Nova and Oneway have safety locks that prevent their jaws from being opened too far (see photo at left). Without such a safety feature, it is easy to inadvertently extend one or more jaws beyond the grip of the scroll. The overextended jaws will fly out of the body when you start the lathe, possibly with deadly consequences. I overextended the jaws of a scroll chuck once with a metal lathe. A 9-lb. jaw ricocheted off the lathe carriage, went through a thermopane window and landed 10 ft. from the building. A metalworker's rule of thumb is to never work with the jaws extended more than halfway out of the chuck body. I have never disobeyed the halfway rule since that sobering experience. Even if the scroll chuck you're using has safety locks, it's still a good idea to test the jaws. Before starting the lathe, test each jaw individually by seeing if it will move, then stand out of the line of fire when you start the lathe.

Spinning jaws are also dangerous. They are real knuckle-busters. Do not to touch (or brush up against) the jaws or chuck body, and be especially wary if the jaws are in the least outside the chuck body. If the job demands working close to the chuck, wrapping the chuck and jaws with duct tape can help. The tape covers sharp edges and helps brush fingers and body parts away rather than being caught by the spinning jaws.

Screw Chucks

A screw chuck is an old favorite for holding small items. What most turners fail to realize is that it can also hold fairly good-size work as well. The design is simplicity itself. A screw protrudes from the face of the chuck. You simply drill a hole in the workpiece the size of the screw, then thread the chuck on the work. Because a right-hand thread opposes the rotation direction of the lathe, the work self-tightens on the chuck. Work can be chucked and unchucked from a screw chuck with fair consistency (a homemade screw chuck is shown on p. 100.

Traditionally, screw chucks are small in size and built on a Morse-taper blank. Such screw chucks are perfect for turning repetitive parts such as drawer pulls or finials. The small screw hole leaves little visible evidence of turning, and with the case of a pull, it facilitates mounting on the finished furniture.

The Glaser screw chuck (left) and the Nova scroll chuck with screw-chuck accessory (middle, back) can hold fairly large work. Traditional screw chucks built on Morse tapers (front middle and right) are for small work.

Drill chucks (also known as Jacobs chucks) are great for mounting drill bits and other accessories in either the tailstock or headstock spindle.

A second type of screw chuck has evolved in recent years. It is built on a faceplate-like body that allows it to be threaded onto the headstock spindle. The more positive drive of the threaded mount allows a really massive screw to be used. Such chucks have a straight screw with a very coarse 45° thread profile. The thread looks much like a giant drywall screw, which makes for a very positive hold. These chucks are good for larger items such as stool seats, lazy Susan's or plant-stand tops. The Glaser screw chuck is of this type, and both the Nova and the Oneway scroll chucks come with screw-chuck accessories with screws of this type (see left photo, above).

Jacobs Chuck

Correctly called a drill chuck, this old stalwart is more often named for the original American manufacturer. In addition to holding drill bits in either the headstock or the tailstock, a drill chuck can successfully hold small work. The drill chuck is also great for mounting buffing wheels in the headstock spindle to make a cheap buffer. Drill chucks are sold according to the largest diameter they can grip. Common sizes are ⅜ in. and ½ in., with the latter being more useful for wood-turning lathes (see right photo, above).

Appendix B
Sharpening Jigs for Grinders

While it's possible to achieve a well-shaped bevel freehand on a grinder, it takes years of practice. For this reason, I strongly recommend that you consider buying one or both of two jigs that aid in the sharpening process. The Glaser Jig and the Oneway sharpening system both allow you to grind correct shapes and angles on turning tools. I have found they allow students to start grinding their own tools the first day of class. And my own tools come out better. When I grind a spindle gouge by eye, there are facets in the edge where I must, of necessity, pause during the grinding process. If I use one of the jigs, I get a perfect fingernail profile.

The Oneway Sharpening System

The Oneway sharpening system is the brainchild of Oneway's driving force, Tim Clay, himself an avid turner. Tim looked at the entire grinding process and came up with some innovative solutions to old sharpening problems. His overall approach balances the grinding wheels easily, dresses the wheels properly and provides jigs for correct sharpening of the tools.

Installing Oneway's hubs and balancing fixture on your grinder wheels eliminates vibration to make grinding easier.

A great impediment to competent grinding is the vibration levels of many bench grinders—especially if the grinder is light in weight. While dressing with a diamond dresser usually improves this situation, it seldom eliminates vibration altogether. If not clamped to the bench, the grinder will "walk" away. The principal culprit here, it turns out, is the average grinding wheel, which is often out of balance.

Oneway sells a set of hubs and a balancing fixture for grinding wheels (see photo at left). The hubs have a series of tapped holes that accept set screws, which serve as counterweights to balance the wheels. The only drawback to Oneway's system is that you'll need grinding wheels with large center holes to accept the Oneway hubs. Such wheels are available at industrial supply stores or directly from Oneway. The package, including the new wheels, will cost around $50 to $100 (depending on the size of your grinder), but it's money well-spent. Oneway suggests balancing the wheel, then dressing it (with their fixture), then balancing it again. The result is that a Canadian faceted penny (which is supplied by Oneway with the balancing weights) will stand on edge on top of the grinder while it's running. Grinding becomes a joy because the machine just sits on the bench and purrs.

The sharpening jig from Oneway (Wolverine) comes with a base unit that mounts under each grinding wheel and an arm that will fit into either base unit (see photo below). There is also a generously sized (3 in. by 5 in.) articulated table that fits into either base unit. This table aids in sharpening plane irons and bench chisels, as well as scrapers. An optional accessory is a clever dressing jig that uses a diamond to dress the wheel dead flat and square.

Two additional jigs for sharpening gouges are available as accessories to use with the Wolverine jig, each one costing around $30. The first is the fingernail jig, which does not, as the name implies, put a fingernail grind on a spindle gouge. The second is the side-grinding jig, which is designed for sharpening bowl gouges, and this

The Wolverine jig from Oneway gives you a base unit to mount under each wheel, a tilting table—which is good for scrapers, plane irons and chisels—and an arm for sharpening roughing-out gouges and for use with the fingernail and side-grinding jigs.

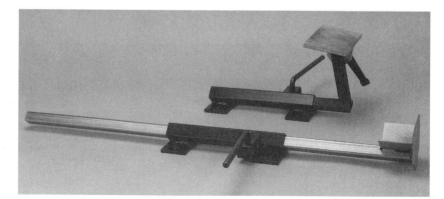

The Oneway side-grinding jig is easy to use and produces a perfect grind on spindle and bowl gouges.

it does very well (see photo above). However, it also gives a better fingernail grind on spindle gouges than the fingernail jig does. I would pass on the fingernail jig altogether and buy only the side-grinding jig. Either jig can be improved by filing the round hole that cradles the tool to a V shape, which will consistently center the tools, especially if they are small in diameter.

To use the jig, clamp a gouge (either spindle or bowl) in the side-grinding jig. To repeat the grind perfectly, the gouge must project out of the jig the same amount each time. You'll need to glue or nail a small block of wood to the bench beside the grinder (or draw a line) to act as a stop (see photo at right). With the grinder off, place the tang of the jig in the pocket at the end of the arm and adjust the arm in or out until you've got the right angle of grind. Then start the grinder and rotate the tool slowly to achieve the desired shape. A perfect shape will be achieved because the tool contacts the wheel perfectly all the time. To easily duplicate a particular grind, mark the correct angle on the arm.

There are some sticky plums in this otherwise tasty pudding, however. The first problem lies with skew chisels. Following Oneway's directions, you achieve a curved hollow grind, which is wretched for architectural turners. The only way I know how to achieve the flat grind is shown on p. 20. The second problem is that the system is designed for a Delta 8-in. grinder, so if you own a 6-in. or 7-in. grinder, you'll have to block up the grinder to the correct height. A 10-in. grinder presents problems in two regards. The base unit does not fit under the wheel, and balancing hubs are not available for shaft sizes larger than ¾ in., and most 10-in. grinders have ⅞ in., or larger,

To repeat a grind perfectly, the gouge must project out of the jig the same amount each time. You can either draw a line or glue or nail a small block of wood to the bench beside the grinder to act as a stop.

shafts. The directions for the system could also do with more illustrations and pictures. For instance, drawings of correct tool profiles would be most helpful.

The Glaser Jig

The Glaser Jig is the contrivance of retired Southern California aerospace engineer, avid turner and craftsman, Jerry Glaser. Jerry was the first to sell a gouge-sharpening jig, and like all the things he designs and makes, it reeks of excellence (see photo below).

Setting up the Glaser Jig demands a grinder at a fixed location, preferably screwed to a bench or fixed to a pedestal. It is necessary to drop a plumb bob from the face of the wheel, then mount a bearing block on the floor a set distance in front of where the plumb bob touches down. This distance is determined by how high your grinder is from the floor, and a chart in the directions calculates this for you (the directions are excellent).

The Glaser Jig helps accomplish a perfect grind on spindle and bowl gouges and offers more flexibility in the shape of the grind than the Oneway side-grinding jig.

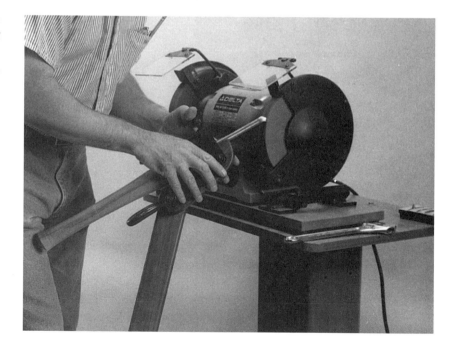

The Glaser Jig was originally designed for sharpening both bowl and spindle gouges, and for this task it offers more flexibility than the Oneway side-grinding Jig. Every aspect of the jig—length of the tang, angle of the gooseneck and distance of the pivot point from the grinding wheel—is adjustable.

It is so adjustable that it takes some patience to get everything set right. A plastic tube is supplied for adjusting the tool position in the jig. Simply slide the tool forward until the tip is even with the end of the tube (see photo at right). Because the tool is clamped in a V-block, perfect alignment and centering is achieved every time. As the flute gets short with age, you'll have to grind a flat spot on the shank to facilitate alignment. Glaser offers a worthwhile accessory that greatly aids the setup process. It is a sample set of gouges, machined into either end of a short mild steel bar. By matching the bevel shape you produce on your tool to the sample tool, you know you are starting with a correct general-purpose grind. You don't grind the sample tool because you make all adjustments with the grinder off. With the sample tool in the jig, adjust everything until both bevels align with the wheel. Now grind the real tool and compare it to the sample tool. Once the right combination of adjustments are found for a grind you like, it is best to mark the jig so that the grind is repeatable.

The jig sharpens spindle gouges well too. Some trial and error is necessary to get things right, and again the sample tool is of great help. The sample spindle gouge has a rather deep flute compared to most spindle gouges. Therefore, some further adjustment of the jig may be necessary if you prefer a gouge with a shallower flute pattern than the sample. The jig also does roughing-out gouges. The system claims to grind skews well, but here again, it's an inappropriate hollow grind and curved edge.

A plastic tube supplied with the Glaser Jig helps get the tool adjusted in the jig. Simply slide the tool forward until the tip is even with the end of the tube.

INDEX

Publisher: *James P. Chiavelli*
Acquisitions editor: *Rick Peters*
Publishing coordinator: *Joanne Renna*
Editor: *Thomas C. McKenna*
Layout Artist: *Lynne Phillips*
Illustrator: *Robert La Pointe*
Indexer: *Diane Sinitsky*
Photographer, except where noted: *Ernie Conover*

Typeface: *Garamond*
Paper: *70 lb. Finch Opaque*
Printer: *Quebecor Printing/Hawkins, New Canton, Tennessee*